PRAISE FOR

# THE CALLING

"GORDON AND CHRIS CHEN tell the amazing ChenMed success story of providing care to the most vulnerable among us. More importantly, they share their 'only in America' journey guided by their faith and family love."

**—JEB BUSH, former Florida Governor
and presidential candidate**

"THE CHENS have taken the concepts of service, hospitality, and excellence and done the impossible—turned healthcare delivery into a world-class, scalable, concierge-level experience for their patients. *The Calling* is a must-read for anyone interested in the future of healthcare and a brighter, healthier, tomorrow."

**—HORST SCHULZE
cofounder, former president, and COO
of The Ritz-Carlton Hotel Company
and author of *Excellence Wins: A No-Nonsense Guide to
Becoming the Best in a World of Compromise***

"A fascinating story of a remarkable family who have overcome great obstacles building a world-changing company. You will be inspired!"

**—BUCK MCCABE, retired EVP and CFO, Chick-fil-A Inc.**

PRAISE *for The* CALLNG

"I FIRST MET DR. CHRIS CHEN when he joined a small group of the most innovative health providers in the country to meet President Obama and discuss what the future of great healthcare should be. Currently, I have the opportunity to see the patient impact of the better medical care delivered at a lower cost to very vulnerable seniors whose lives are improved every day by having access to a ChenMed physician.

The Chen family of providers are working hard to erase the inequities of our current health system. Their goal—and their calling—is to transform care delivery so that better care at a lower cost is available to the more-vulnerable Americans. The mission is both inspirational and meaningful, and *The Calling* is an important book for anyone interested in better healthcare in America."

**—KATHLEEN SEBELIUS**
**former Secretary of the US Department**
**of Health and Human Services, 2009–2014**

"A WONDERFUL READ. Chris and Gordon share a deeply moving story of their family's mission to change the course of healthcare in America by making it kinder, simpler, more personal—the kind of care everyone wishes for their loved ones. What makes their story so compelling is they've brought this mission to life, making personalized, empathetic, and holistic care a reality for hundreds of thousands of people. Our country is better off for their persistence and passion for the cause."

**—BRUCE D. BROUSSARD**
**president & CEO, Humana Inc.**

"A MUST-READ for every American, *The Calling* details how we as a nation can build a more compassionate and affordable healthcare system for all. In fact, they've already started changing the lives of millions of people—a model that continues to blossom across the country. It is winning people over and challenging the status quo medical establishment."

— **DR. MARTY MAKARY,** Johns Hopkins professor and *New York Times* best-selling author of *The Price We Pay*

"*THE CALLING* tells the inspirational story of the Chen family, which over two generations not only completed the American Dream but also transformed American medicine. Their narrative shines a bright light on the problems of the current healthcare system and the power of purpose, focus, and faith to solve them. It is a must-read for anyone who has lost hope in the medical profession."

—**ROBERT PEARL, M.D.**
**Stanford University School of Medicine and Business and author of** *Uncaring: How the Culture of Medicine Kills Doctors & Patients*

"THE BOOK is an amazing story of two brothers, their wives, and the family's commitment to service and excellent patient care for the most underserved. From Taiwan to Miami, the family's story shows what faith, purpose, setting high expectations, and family can achieve. The ChenMed model of care stands out as a beacon to move the country from sick care to truly meeting a patient's needs. My hope is that there are many followers. Patients are waiting."

— **RON WILLIAMS,** former chairman and CEO of AETNA, Inc. and best-selling author of *Learning to Lead*

PRAISE *for The* CALLNG

"THE LIFE EXPERIENCES that shape not one but two generations of innovative leaders in healthcare compel this inspiring story of how ChenMed came to be one of the beacons of value-driven care in the nation. In this refreshingly honest family business memoir, Chris and Gordon Chen pay tribute to their parents, Dr. James and Mary Chen, as well as their wives, friends, and all who have guided them. *The Calling* shows how their unwavering compunction to serve those in the greatest need like their own family, together with their deep faith, have guided their decisions and led to their success. This is their origin story, and we eagerly await the sequel."

— **DR. VIVIAN S. LEE**
author of *The Long Fix: Solving America's
Health Care Crisis with Strategies
that Work for Everyone*

"THIS BOOK OFFERS guidance on faith and family, personal and business development, dealing with setbacks, and making the most of opportunities. If you let it, *The Calling: A Memoir of Family, Faith, and the Future of Healthcare* will challenge you and also help you find your unique place in your family and in the world. Along the way, you'll be called to make your relationships at work and home stronger and more centered on a vision of a better future. For those of us called to heal healthcare, we'll see that only a company informed by thousands of years of family and spiritual wisdom is up to that monumental task—and you'll want help!"

—**DAVE LOGAN, PHD,** *New York Times*
best-selling co-author of *Tribal Leadership,*
cofounder of three businesses
including Care4th, and professor
at the USC Marshall School of Business

## PRAISE for The CALLNG

"WHAT A FANTASTIC STORY this is! A family-run business trying to improve healthcare for some of the most underserved populations in the nation. They have managed to finance the enterprise on their own and are now poised with a great foundation of successful clinics to expand rapidly. This is truly a story that deserves to be studied and better appreciated."

**—HERBERT FRITCH, founder and CEO of HealthSpring**

"*THE CALLING* shows how the stories of a great immigrant family and a transformational healthcare organization begin with strong values and simple commitments—e.g., respect your parents and see every patient every month. While the stories are intertwined, the authors have learned over time of the distinction between unconditional family relationships and conditional business relationships. Their insights can help organizations of all types thrive through the performance of noble work during our tumultuous times."

**—THOMAS LEE, M.D., chief medical officer, Press Ganey Associates and author of *The Good Doctor***

"THIS BOOK CHRONICLES the trials and successes of a family that have their priorities straight. The Chens put faith and service first. This book is about everything that's right in healthcare."

**—A. MARC HARRISON, M.D. president and CEO, Intermountain Healthcare**

"THE CHEN FAMILY have created a national model for high touch, efficient, and effective healthcare serving the most vulnerable seniors. Clinically-led and patient-centered, value-based care models are the road map necessary for a sustainable high quality care system for all of America."

**—ROBERT MARGOLIS, M.D. founder of the Duke-Margolis Center for Health Policy and current advisory board chairman**

# THE
# CALLING

# THE
# CALLING

## A MEMOIR OF FAMILY, FAITH, AND THE FUTURE OF HEALTHCARE

### Dr. CHRIS CHEN AND
### Dr. GORDON CHEN

FOREWORD BY
JOHN C. MAXWELL

Forefront
BOOKS

Library of Congress Control Number: 2022909301

ISBN: 978-1-63763-115-7 (Print)
ISBN: 978-1-63763-116-4 (eBook)

Cover Design by Bruce Gore, GORE STUDIO, INC.
Interior Design by Mary Susan Oleson, BLU DESIGN CONCEPTS
Cover photo by Rick Luettke, LUETTKE STUDIO INC.

WE DEDICATE THIS BOOK
TO OUR PARENTS, WIVES, AND CHILDREN

*Mom and Dad, we thank you
for your endless love, timeless wisdom,
and persevering faith.*

*To our precious wives, thank you
for being our biggest supporters.
We deeply love you and appreciate
how you make us better husbands,
fathers, leaders, and men of faith.
We thank God for you every day.*

*To our dearly loved children,
you are so special both individually and together.
We pray you invest in and pass
our values down to future generations.*

# TABLE of CONTENTS

# FOREWORD

## JOHN C. MAXWELL

---

WHEN I WAS ASKED to write this foreword for Drs. Chris and Gordon Chen's book, I was intrigued. They are doing something in healthcare that is remarkable and courageous.

Not many healthcare professionals have the expertise, faith, and determination to take on the multibillion-dollar industry in which they operate. But that's exactly what the Chens are doing, and in the process they are accelerating the transformation of healthcare in America. They are also touching many people in a deep and personal way. It is inspiring.

Their book *The Calling: A Memoir of Faith, Family, and the Future of Healthcare* is a story of how a family of deep faith persevered through trials and challenges to emerge stronger, more passionate, and more focused. They are leading a healthcare revolution and transforming a broken healthcare system. Their story must be shared.

I have always said leadership is influence—nothing more, nothing less. As Chris and Gordon have grown personally and professionally, so has their influence. They have used their influence to improve the health of their patients, help doctors to achieve a greater purpose, and improve their healthcare culture to achieve scalable outcomes.

Chris and Gordon have embraced my book *The 5 Levels of Leadership*, and *The Calling* will be their Pinnacle level calling card. They are developing a leadership culture at ChenMed with the goal of providing something better for clinicians and the underserved senior citizens in communities across America. Their vision is to be America's leading primary care provider, transforming care for the neediest populations. They are well on their way to achieving this goal.

I've spent time getting to know Chris, Gordon, and their families. I am inspired by their faith and devotion to the senior citizens they wholeheartedly serve. They talk about building a multigenerational healthcare ministry that will transform healthcare and bring light to the underserved. I have no doubt they will succeed in record time.

Their book will make you laugh, cry, and call you toward a brighter future for American healthcare. It will also touch your heart in a deep and meaningful way and draw you toward their family purpose, to glorify God by spreading more love and better health in all whom they encounter. From their near-death experiences and business struggles to a brighter future where everyone wins, you will be glad they shared their journey with you.

—JOHN C. MAXWELL
*Best-Selling Author and Founder Maxwell Leadership®*

# A NOTE from YOUR AUTHORS

OUR FAMILY HAS BEEN called on a mission. We received our calling through our faith, and this calling has put us on a path to change how healthcare is delivered in America and transform lives among the neediest populations.

We start our story where it must: with our parents and family. Our parents came to this country with nothing except their dreams and values. Without them, we would never have created the company we did. So we'll introduce Dad, Mom, our wives, and even our children. We'll tell you stories that not only give you a sense of who we are, but also show how we became people capable of executing such a revolutionary vision for healthcare in America.

There are three components of our story—family, faith, and a commitment to make a positive impact on healthcare for the most vulnerable among us. All three components are inextricably intertwined in who we are as people and how we live our lives.

*The Calling* is a story of healthcare transformation. Far too many people experience decreasing healthcare results that cost more money and increase inequity. As a family, we've created a proven solution that addresses both issues—our system delivers improved health for less money and rectifies inequities at the same time.

You can read our book as another great American success story or you can read it as the story of two sons who honor their parents as role models and who are committed to extending their legacy from one generation to the next. You can even read it as the story of two daughters-in-law who have embraced their roles as members of our family and as agents of healthcare change.

But no matter how you read *The Calling*, please read it as *our* story: a family of doctors whose lives are intertwined as parents, siblings, in-laws, business partners, and people of faith. We, Chris and Gordon, just happen to be your guides through the Chen family journey.

Telling this story together presented us with a funny, and interesting, challenge.

The funny part is that people already mistake us for each other all the time. We are two very tall Chinese brothers born a few years apart who both happen to be doctors. People say we even sound alike. So if people who know us often are confused about who they're listening to, what chance do you have? That was our challenge.

We didn't want to write an entire book saying, "Hey, this is Chris talking," or "I'm Gordon telling this story." So when we could we used the pronoun "we." Of course, when one of us had to plan a wedding in twenty-four hours or the other got COVID, for example, we refer to each other in the third person. That way there's no doubt who was involved in the event. But for less specific events we opted for an approach that's easier to read.

Perhaps you'll get a kick out of just how inextricably intertwined we are. Not only do the two of us work together as Chief Executive Officer and Chief Medical Officer of ChenMed, we live with our wives, Stephanie and Jessica, along with our eight children (each of us has four) and our parents on the same street in three houses in a row—lot line to lot line to lot line. We're one family, sharing one faith, on one mission, and we love living life to the fullest *together*.

Now, here's our story.

CHAPTER 1

# ONE WEDDING and an (ALMOST) FUNERAL

"I NEED YOU to pick me up," our dad said.

It sounds like such a simple request—to have Dad ask either one of us for a ride. Gordon, at that time a third-year medical student serving a clerkship in psychiatry at Jackson Memorial Hospital in Miami, received this call on September 29, 2003. Under normal circumstances, it would be an innocuous and relatively easy request to fulfill. But for our dad to make that call, and for the reason he needed to make it, it was generationally life-changing for our family, our medical center, and potentially millions of patients whose lives will be positively influenced by what followed.

One week prior, our father had visited with Chris, the older of us and already a doctor, and his wife, Stephanie, in New York City. Chris was in the first year of his fellowship in cardiology at Cornell University Medical College. Dad casually mentioned that he was experiencing some numbness in his face, particularly just above the left side of his mouth. It didn't seem like too big a deal, but Chris encouraged him to have it checked. At the time, Chris thought it might be a condition called *hypocalcemia,* a calcium deficiency. Calcium disturbances are known to cause numbness around the mouth.

As it turned out, however, it was a very, very big deal. After getting evaluated by both his dentist and his ear, nose, and throat (ENT) physician, a subsequent CT scan changed everything. Resilient and strong, a stoic survivor never shaken by anything life threw at him, our father was so upset by the news he received that after reviewing the preliminary results of the CT scan, he called Gordon to drive him home.

"Gordon, I have a big mass behind my nose, and I can't drive. I need you to pick me up."

For Gordon, time slowed down. There was an immediate shift from carefree medical student who only had to worry about upcoming exams to a concerned son scrambling to figure out the next steps to help Dad survive. He and his fiancée, Jessica, took the CT scan images to be reviewed by top neuroradiologists at the University of Miami and found out the tumor was enmeshed in very sensitive tissue, growing back toward Dad's brain, involving vessels and muscle. This tumor was impinging on one of his nerves, causing the numbness on his lip. A subsequent biopsy revealed that the mass growing behind his nose was a squamous cell cancer, an insidious form of cancer treated in just one way—it must be cut out. No chemotherapy, no radiation. But this wasn't a nicely formed, easy-to-remove tumor. Only a very dangerous operation could remove it. And even if Dad survived such a surgery, given the nature of what the oncologist and pathologist had discovered about the size and location of the tumor, the prognosis was grim.

Dad also called our mother, Mary, and told her about the cancer. She knew it was serious, but because she didn't have the medical knowledge her sons and husband possessed, she didn't understand the full impact of what we were facing. Dad did not tell her the prognosis: he had been told this was a terminal mass. He probably only had two months to live. Still, she called Chris in New York to tell him the news.

"Chris, your father has cancer," she said. "You need to come home and take care of your family."

We're not sure how much of her words and Chris's response is based on our Chinese cultural heritage and how much is simply our unique family dynamic. Both of us were raised to honor and respect the wishes of our parents, and both our mom and dad have proven to be two people worthy of honor and respect. In this particular situation, Chris had total faith that Mom would never ask anything of him that wasn't necessary and best for all of us.

A whirlwind of activity and strategies for dealing with the situation ensued. First and foremost, our entire family turned to prayer. We determined to take it one day at a time, one step at a time, trusting God to lead and guide us. As soon as he could, Chris met with his cardiology fellowship director.

In Chris's mind, there was no other decision to be made—he intended to resign from his fellowship and return home sooner than expected to learn how to run the medical center that our father and mother had worked so hard to build. In that meeting, however, the director refused to accept his resignation.

"Don't do anything rash, Chris," he said. "Go home, get a full assessment of the situation, do what you need to do for your family, and come back. I do not want you to resign. We will make this work."

Chris learned later that his mentor had recently gotten a diagnosis of prostate cancer and, as it turned out, had just two years to live himself. He was extremely empathetic with Chris and the family situation, and he was willing to do whatever he and the program could to accommodate our needs.

Stephanie, in her second year of law school in New York, immediately went to discuss the family's situation with her dean. She asked for a year's deferment to be able to go back to South Florida to help with Dad's care. After Stephanie explained what she wanted to do, the dean seemed surprised and questioned her.

"This isn't even your father," he said. "Are you sure you want to do this for your father-in-law?"

"I'm sure," Stephanie explained. "This man is no ordinary father-in-law!"

After that meeting, she called Chris from a cab on the way to the airport. She had gotten her deferment, would not lose any of her grants or scholarships, and was on her way to Miami to do whatever she could for our family.

"I'll meet you there when you finish your rotation and can get a flight out," she said.

Chris stayed in New York one more day to complete his Wednesday responsibilities at the hospital, then flew out the next day.

Meanwhile, he started looking for the best person in the world to turn to for a second opinion and to perform the surgery. After reaching out to everyone who might be able to help among his Harvard, Beth Israel, and Sloan Kettering connections, Chris identified an ear, nose, and throat oncology surgeon at MD Anderson in Houston, Texas.

In the meantime, problems had arisen with the doctors back home. First, we were told that the earliest appointment with an oncologist was six weeks away. Considering that Dad had been given a prognosis of two months to live, we were incredulous that anyone would think that acceptable. Six different oncologists offered us uncoordinated, conflicting responses. Frustration hit an explosive level when we were stonewalled by the pathologist, whom we considered a family friend, after we asked for a tissue block, a biopsied sample from the mass, to send off to MD Anderson for testing. It seemed that the local pathologist was offended and didn't want us to get a second opinion. We were united, however, and refused to take "No" for an answer. Finally, on Friday, after Chris exerted great pressure, a block was released and sent overnight by FedEx to Houston, where Dad had an appointment with the surgeon on Monday morning. Together we decided that Dad and Gordon would fly out on Sunday afternoon.

GORDON AND JESSICA, who was in her second year at the University of Miami Miller School of Medicine, had planned their wedding for later that same year during the Christmas break, on December 20. They had gotten to know one another through a faith-based medical association, and on a medical mission trip to Nicaragua in the spring they really had begun to connect. When they had gotten back home, they had been practically inseparable, studying together for medical school exams, exercising together daily, and praying together every night. Gordon told her four weeks later that he planned to marry her. Her response?

"I know."

When they had talked with our mom and dad about their plans to get married, Mom had asked Jessica, "Do you want a traditional American wedding, where the bride's family covers the costs, or a traditional Chinese wedding, where the groom's family foots the bill?"

Jessica had made a quick decision. "I like the Chinese approach!"

Our mom, the most generous person you will ever meet, had given them a budget of $30,000 for the wedding, which they could spend any way they wished, and they could keep whatever they didn't spend. The news about our dad, however, required flexibility.

In talking with the ENT surgeon at MD Anderson, Chris learned that the surgery involved removing Dad's face, including taking out his eyes and eye orbit, his nose, part of his jawline, and then recreating his face using bones from his legs. In all likelihood, even that extreme surgery might only buy him six more months. And if he survived the operation and lived until the wedding in December, what sort of shape would our father be in, and would he ever look like himself again? Chris remembers seeing a hospice pamphlet on Dad's desk. Was he seriously considering not going through with the surgery? How long would he have to live without it? Gordon and Jessica, and of course, Mom and Dad, desperately wanted Dad to be at their wedding. With Dad's encouragement, Mom spoke to Gordon about the situation on Thursday evening, October 2.

"Gordon, considering what we as a family are facing with your father, we don't want any ambiguity," she said. "December 20 is too far away—will your father be with us then? How will his recovery process go? We have no idea what life will be like in December. We know it's asking a lot, but would you talk with Jessica about moving the date up? And could you make it *this weekend?*"

On Friday morning, Gordon called Jessica and asked if she would get married the next day. She didn't hesitate. That allowed them twenty-four hours to get both families in town from all over the country (plus one of Jessica's sisters, who was on vacation with friends in the Bahamas), secure a marriage license, the church, the officiant, tuxedos, bridesmaids' dresses, and a wedding dress for Jessica. The bridesmaids' dresses and wedding dress had been ordered but weren't supposed to be ready until much closer to the December 20 date.

Impossible, right? No. A miracle happened.

Our family's spiritual home, First Baptist Church of Fort Lauderdale, a large church with weddings booked almost every weekend, *just so happened* to be available Saturday, October 4. On Friday morning, Jessica called the boutique where she had ordered the bridesmaid dresses to learn they were not in yet.

"Please, check again. I'm getting married tomorrow," Jessica implored the owner, who was a longtime family friend.

They called back shortly after to say the dresses had arrived—much, much earlier than they were expected. Jessica already had her wedding dress, but it hadn't been altered yet. Countless phone calls produced booked flights that would get almost everyone from both families to Miami in time for a Saturday afternoon ceremony. Jessica had no idea where her sister was staying in the Bahamas or who exactly she was with. She went to bed Friday evening thinking her sister would not make it in time, but the next morning one of her brothers phoned to say that he had tracked their sister down at 2:00 a.m. and gotten her a flight that morning to Miami. Everyone would be there.

Stephanie's mother spent Saturday morning arranging flowers from a local supermarket and ordering a beautiful wedding cake for the reception. Jessica's mom spent the day with a needle and thread, putting darts in the wedding dress and bridesmaids' dresses to keep them up, using double-sided tape to hem them. Our pastor, Larry Thompson, helped Gordon and Jessica get their marriage license in time for the ceremony. He also said that the pianist and a Grammy Award–winning vocalist were performing for free, and there would be no charge for anything the church could provide for the wedding and reception afterward.

Mom likes to laugh now at the financial deal the Lord worked out for Jessica and Gordon!

We were a rather somber group, however, as we gathered at the church to prepare for the ceremony. While Gordon was thrilled to be marrying his partner for life, he was also trying to prepare mentally for what would happen at MD Anderson two days later.

Pastor Thompson pulled Gordon aside shortly before leading him and the groomsmen into the church. "Gordon, you have a choice to make right now," he said, "and you only have one chance to make that choice."

Gordon looked at him, wondering what he meant. Pastor Thompson continued.

"There are two doors in this room. You can go out that one"—he pointed to the door that led outside the church— "and continue with your life as a single man. But if you go out this other one with us"—and here he pointed to the door that led into the church—"there's no turning back. Your life will never be the same."

Gordon knew he was half serious and half kidding.

"I'm going with you, Pastor," he said.

While they were having this conversation, we received our second miracle of the week.

Chris, who, along with Dad, was one of Gordon's best men, felt his phone vibrate in his pocket. He looked and saw it was a Houston number so he took the call. The physician in charge of head and neck cancers at MD Anderson, who specialized in the type and location of Dad's cancer, had gone into work that Saturday morning. He went down to the FedEx dock and sorted through two hundred boxes, found the one with Dad's cell block (the biopsied tissue), and rushed to put the sample under his microscope. He couldn't wait to give Chris the news.

"Chris, Chris, let me tell you something!" Of Greek heritage, he had a strong, dynamic, wonderful personality, and Chris could tell he was excited about what he had found.

"I got your slides," he said. "I'm looking at this right now, and I know what the other pathologist told you. I can sort of see why they might have thought this was squamous cell. But I don't think so. I have to confirm it, but I think this is a weird kind of B-cell, non-Hodgkin's lymphoma that we've seen before. I'm pretty sure I'm right!"

Chris knew what it meant if he was right. He grabbed Dad and hugged him.

"Dad, there's hope! He thinks it's lymphoma!"

"Oh, thank God! Thank God!" Dad said. A doctor himself, he also understood immediately the difference this could make.

As Pastor Thompson started to lead us into the church, Dad leaned forward to whisper into Gordon's ear.

"Gordon, the doctor in Houston thinks it's B-cell lymphoma!"

Gordon could barely take in what Dad was saying. He had just finished a part-funny, part-challenging conversation with our pastor about one of the biggest decisions he would ever make in his life, and now he was hearing that our father may have a more hopeful prognosis.

"Praise the Lord!" he said as the news sank in, understanding what it meant, and hugged Dad.

We got the news to Mom, and it spread quickly throughout the wedding party. We knew that a mass like Dad's, if squamous cell, was terminal. But if it truly was lymphatic cancer, then it would be treatable with chemo and radiation. While lymphoma grows extremely fast, that rapid growth also makes it more susceptible to chemo. The chemo poisons the cancer cells, and they "eat up" the poison faster as they spread and grow.

This new diagnosis wasn't a guarantee of a much longer life, but if correct, it gave us what we desperately needed—hope. And we were more than happy and thankful to God to grab on to that hope with everything we had.

For Gordon and Jessica, that news was the best wedding present they could have imagined. Yes, we all joyfully celebrated God's blessing of their union as husband and wife that day, but we had much more to celebrate as family and friends on a beautiful fall Saturday. The church was filled with members of the congregation who were praying for our dad, along with almost the entire medical school that had heard what was happening with Gordon and Jessica. The newly married couple's "honeymoon" was to last but one night—Gordon left his bride the next day to fly out to Houston with Dad.

Before the newlyweds left that Sunday afternoon, all

the family gathered at the church to worship together. Pastor Thompson invited Dad to the front of the church and anointed him with oil, asking God to fulfill a biblical promise of healing. The whole church prayed over Dad and sent Gordon and him off to Houston. Pastor Thompson didn't stop with prayer. He flew to Houston and spent the first few days with Dad and Gordon, making sure they were settled in and well taken care of. What an encouragement and blessing this man of God was for us throughout this ordeal!

THE FRIDAY BEFORE the wedding, Chris had spent all day with Dad, a composition notebook and small recorder in his hands, trying to get a crash course on how to run the medical center. It had been the plan since Chris was a young boy. Dad had come home from medical school one day and said, "Chris, you're going to go to Miami's six-year medical program, go away for more schooling, then come back so we can work together." Chris was five years old at the time.

That had been the family dream for decades. We had no idea how that dream would become a reality much quicker than planned, and on that Friday, the dream seemed more like a nightmare. Given the risk we were facing, we didn't know if he would survive the operation. Since Dad was leaving on Sunday for MD Anderson to meet with the surgeon on Monday, Chris might have had *only* that one day for Dad to teach him how to run the medical center. Chris recalls writing things down that he didn't understand and thinking, *I'll come back to this later and hopefully figure it out.*

Chris begged our father to let him be the one to go with him to MD Anderson.

"No, son. Your job is here," he said. "You take care of Mommi, my patients, and the business. Gordon will go with me. This medical center not only supports your family. It also supports and provides care for many others. It pays for what I need and for what our family needs. Let Gordon and me take care of what happens in Houston."

That's why Gordon went with Dad to Houston the day after his wedding to meet with the ENT surgeon, our entryway into the MD Anderson system. Once there, the pathologist in Houston confirmed that it was lymphoma, not squamous cell.

The war was far from over, however. A new battle plan had to be drawn. When Gordon and Dad went to MD Anderson, they only had the appointment with an ENT surgeon, and we had just discovered we needed a medical oncologist. Their first week there, they pleaded with schedulers, called any contacts they knew, and desperately prayed for help. Finally, they were able to get on the schedule of Dr. Jorge Romaguerra, one of the top medical oncologists at MD Anderson.

A plan was quickly put into place, and after a battery of testing and consultations, Dr. Romaguerra mapped out a regimen that included months of two forms of chemotherapy, which would be followed by six weeks of radiation. First on the schedule was a series of six three-week R-chop chemotherapy treatments. Because of the location of the mass and the fact that it had already begun to affect Dad's cranial nerves, which was causing the numbness in his upper lip, he also needed intrathecal chemotherapy—treatments injected directly into his spinal fluid to attack the cancer there.

Gordon and Dad were incredibly busy that first week, gathering records, going from test to consultant to test, with what felt like endless waiting in between—a bone marrow biopsy, labs, a stress test, a MUGA scan, consultations with cardiology, dental, and radiation oncology, then more labs and spinal taps. Mom joined Dad and Gordon in Houston on the third day just as they were preparing to place his tunneled central venous catheter (also known as a "central line") in preparation for his chemotherapy.

The first doctor struggled to get Dad's central line in, likely due to Dad's scoliosis. Dad believes his curved spine was a result of his early years in China, where his family was very poor. He was malnourished, and he had to help his mother by carrying his mentally disabled younger brother on his back.

When the third attempt to insert the central line did not work, the nurse told Mom they were going to have to discharge Dad without it. Mom was having none of that! She knew it would delay his treatment, and every moment was precious and necessary to stop the growth of this mass before it did more damage.

"We're not going anywhere until he gets that central line," she told the nurse who had said they were releasing him.

The nurse called Dad's primary doctor at MD Anderson and told him that our mom and dad were refusing to leave. He called in another doctor, who happened to be Chinese, to try again. On his first try, Dad's central line was inserted, and he was ready for chemo to begin. Everyone was so thankful that his catheter was in place for chemo. This was the access to life-saving chemotherapy that could stop the growth of the tumor.

Mom flew back home once she was assured that the catheter was working, knowing she was the only full-time person running the family business. Gordon and Dad stayed together in Houston to complete his first cycle of chemotherapy. Once that first round was completed, Gordon and Dad returned home after ten days away. Though the family knew there were still many challenges ahead, we had reached the first major milestone toward healing. We also had a clear sign that all the prayers were being answered.

WHILE DAD AND GORDON were busy in Houston, Chris was able to work out a schedule with his cardiology fellowship in which he would spend four days in New York, Sunday night through Thursday, fulfilling his duties there. That phrase *fulfilling his duties there* meant fitting in eighty hours of cardiology rotation in four days. He would then fly home to spend Friday running the medical center and taking care of Dad's patients, Saturday doing whatever was necessary, and then being with the family and going to church on Sunday.

During the week, Mom handled the business and administrative aspects of the medical center. Chris dove into understanding the medical and patient care components. Unlike many family businesses in which the patriarch or matriarch who starts the business has difficulty letting go of control and the next generation may or may not be interested in keeping the business going, our whole family was fully invested in making sure that we did everything we could to help Dad beat cancer *and* that the medical center was prepared for success. What happened during that time paved the way for what we could only hope and imagine ChenMed would eventually become.

From his days at Beth Israel, Chris had a friend, Bob Kocher, who had been at McKinsey, a top management consulting firm, before completing his medical degree. When Bob heard what was happening with our dad and that Chris was trying to learn the business side of medical practice, he called to offer his help

"Chris, I understand you're now running your dad's practice," he said. "As a doctor who is also McKinsey-trained, I can help. Just let me know what you need from me, and I'm there."

He essentially wound up giving Chris the equivalent of an MBA with the business training he offered, teaching him how to think from a business perspective. Bob was also highly impressed by the business model Dad had created for the medical center; it was at this point Chris realized we had something unique to offer the medical community and their patients. The patients we serve are older, poor, and very sick— the underserved, the patients no other doctors want. Dad's plan allowed him to take care of these patients, who were being sent to him by other practices, and still have a profitable business model.

Throughout his treatments, Dad poured his energy into surviving, first and foremost, and then analyzing the data on the medical center. How could things be run better, not only for the business aspect of what we were doing, but especially to make it the best it could be for the patients we were serving?

Dad's concern for the well-being of his patients was not new. Chris recalls that Friday, when he thought he had but one day to learn how to run the medical center, Dad expressed special compassion for several patients.

"Chris, you must not forget to follow up on this," Dad said. "I'm worried about what's going on with these patients."

Chris remembers thinking at the time—*Why in the heck are you worrying about these people when you are going to die? You just need to take care of yourself!* The same love for others that drove our father to damage his spine when he was a young boy in China, carrying his younger brother around on his back, motivated him to think about the care of his patients when he had gotten a terminal diagnosis himself.

The chemotherapy, while it was attacking the cancer cells, also wiped out Dad's immune system. This meant he had to live in a bubble—any little thing that came in contact with his system could kill him. We put ICU filters in every room of the apartment we rented for him in Houston and constantly scrubbed everything down. When the COVID-19 pandemic hit in 2020, taking special care with hygiene and quarantining was nothing new for Dad and the rest of our family!

Once Dad was situated and had started his treatments, Chris's wife, Stephanie, stepped up. Having gotten a full-year deferral at her law school, she volunteered to stay in Houston with Dad during his first several rounds of chemotherapy, which had to take place there, and help with his care. After those first rounds of the six he would undergo, we were able to work it out for MD Anderson to send the treatments to a hospital near our home. Dad didn't have to stay in Houston the entire time.

It wasn't too long after he was back home that we had our first major setback. Mom, Dad, Jessica, and Gordon were all watching a Miami Dolphins football game. Chris and Stephanie had gone out to a restaurant for a rare date. Dad had been suffering from a really bad headache for a few days, which had gotten worse that day. Yelling at the Dolphins for their poor play didn't help! When Dolphin quarterback Jay Fiedler threw his second interception of the game, Dad had a seizure—his arm began to shake uncontrollably and he couldn't speak. Gordon was in the middle of a neurology rotation, and he immediately began processing what was happening with our father. He knew it wasn't good.

They got Dad to the emergency room, where the medical team ran a CT scan and other tests to see what was going on. It turned out that he was leaking spinal fluid from a prior spinal tap, and that was causing a severe headache. To relieve the pain causing his headache, he had lowered his head. But that caused the blood around the central line in his neck to clot, eventually building up pressure in his jugular vein and causing a little blood to leak into his brain, which triggered the seizure. Chris and Stephanie arrived at the hospital to find Dad in the ICU. Chris called his friends in New York and Boston to ask what should be done.

"Chris, you've got to put him on blood thinners," they said.

"What? Didn't you hear me?" Chris said. "He has bleeding in his brain!"

It sounds counterintuitive, but they explained that the bleed was caused by blood clots, which can form when you have cancer. They told him there was a risk—the treatment could cause even more bleeding in the brain and kill Dad. But without alleviating the pressure from the blood clots, he definitely would die. We took their advice, as risky as it was.

There was one story from that first night in the ICU that we can laugh about now as a family. Dad kept complaining about a smell—an awful smell. None of the rest of us smelled it. Chris thought that the seizure or the bleeding in his brain was creating an artificially bad smell that wasn't there. Dad referred to the smell several times in the early evening. The rest of the family left, but Chris stayed to spend the night in the room with Dad to monitor how he was doing with the blood thinners. Just as Dad was falling off to sleep, he said:

"Chris, even though you smell so bad, I still love you."

Chris thought, *These could be my dad's dying words to me!*

The next morning, Stephanie arrived. Dad, who had survived the night (thank God!), told her that Chris really needed to go home and take a shower—he smelled so bad. Chris looked at her as if to say, *I don't know what he's smelling, but it isn't me!*

Stephanie, ever the practical one, walked over to Dad's bed.

"Let me see your pillow," she said, and smelled it.

"Oh, my gosh!" she went on. "Someone must have thrown up on this pillow, and it never got switched out. Is this what you were smelling, Dad? This is horrible!"

Dad wound up spending five days in ICU, a few more days in the hospital, and then was finally able to return home. We all had quite a scare.

It's FUNNY what we think about during life's worst moments. Dad was battling cancer, and Chris and Stephanie decided to try for a baby. They were originally going to wait until Chris finished his cardiology fellowship to have children, but they wanted to tell Dad that his legacy would continue into the next generation. Within a week, the baby, James (named after Dad), was on the way. On Christmas Day that year, they were able to give Dad a very special present. They handed him a sonogram image of the baby she was carrying. Dad kept it in his room for many, many years.

After the six rounds of chemotherapy were completed, Dad had to return to an apartment in Houston to begin the radiation treatments at MD Anderson. Stephanie again was there with Dad, staying with him Sunday evening through Thursday, cooking, doing laundry, making sure he did his exercises, and doing whatever she could to help.

The help between them was not just in one direction. As Stephanie grew bigger and bigger during her first two trimesters, she needed maternity clothes. Dad would go shopping with her, wearing a mask (before that became common) and a hat to cover his baldness from chemotherapy. She would try something on and step out of the dressing room to ask if it looked OK.

"Stephanie, Mom says I have no sense of fashion or style," Dad said. "You should do the opposite of whatever I think!"

Stephanie remembers laughing so hard at that, while being thankful that she had a father-in-law who cared about her and wanted to go shopping with her, even though he was so sick. He showed his generosity, love, and kindness in other ways during their time together. Every day, he asked her what she wanted. He'd always have her make the decision, whether that was the cuisine and menu for dinner, the restaurant or takeout they would choose, the movie or art museum they would attend, or the park activity they would engage in. "You are pregnant," said Dad. "You get to pick."

During her break from medical school, Jessica also helped out in Houston. She and Stephanie baked cakes and cookies to take to the nurses at the hospital. This, along with buying lunch for the entire oncology department several times, may have helped ensure Dad got first-class care. Mom flew out to be with him Friday through Sunday for the first four weeks of radiation.

During those long weekends, Mom never ran into Dad's doctor. Finally, when she went out to stay with Dad for the last two weeks of radiation, she met his doctor. His first question to her was not about Dad's condition or how she and the family were doing with all of this.

"How do you have such good daughters-in-law?" asked the doctor.

Mom smiled. "God is very good to us," she explained.

Yes, He is. As a family, we have no doubt about that.

WHILE WE WERE ENGAGED in Dad's physical battle with cancer, there was a spiritual battle being waged as well. Mom struggled daily with God, like David in the Psalms or Jacob wrestling with God on his way to Canaan. It's an almost universal question for anyone of faith, and one with no easy answers—*Why does a loving God allow such human suffering?* Many tears were shed—more than either of us had ever seen from this stalwart woman who had weathered so much buffeting from life's storms throughout her life.

Chris remembers crying out to God, through his tears, the day he learned of Dad's cancer. He tried to strike a bargain. "God, if you will save my dad, I promise I'll climb to the mountaintops to shout out what You have done!"

We're usually in deep trouble when we start trying to bargain with the Creator of the universe. Still, God was faithful, and so were many others who prayed for Dad from the very beginning. Mom learned of a prayer chain group, stretching all across the world, of people of faith praying for Dad and our family.

A longtime family friend from church and leader of the prayer chain, Sharon Brody, called Mom every day to ask how Dad was doing. She used the analogy of the children of Israel crossing the Red Sea when she reached out to ask how they should be praying.

"Where are we today?" she would ask. "How much progress have we made? What percentage do we have to go to get to the other side?"

"We're ten percent across," Mom would say. And as the

days, weeks, and months went by, we got closer and closer to the Promised Land.

The necessity of doing everything she could to keep the medical center running as a business helped Mom focus her mind on what she needed to do, rather than worry about the what-ifs of Dad's health. More significant than busyness, however, was her faith in God. That and the prayers of the saints got them—got us all—through this difficult time.

Cancer, disease, injuries, death—these are not good things. But our God is a good God who can take the awful things that life throws at us and bring something good out of them.

"We must offer our patients the type of care you were able to offer me," Dad told us.

As we thought about what he was saying, we realized a profound truth. Very, very few people have the resources to accomplish what we were able to do for our father—a family with four medical professionals who were able to draw from the best resources the American medical community has to offer: a wife who is a crusader, unwilling to accept "No" for an answer, and a daughter-in-law who is able and willing to give her full attention to him. How many people have contacts at Harvard, Beth Israel, Sloan Kettering, and MD Anderson? Even with all of that, ours was an arduous, soul-wrenching journey. How much more difficult must it be for the older, underserved patients God was sending us? We began to understand we needed to pour the same energy into meeting the needs of our patients that we exerted for our father.

In late June 2004, Dad knew that he was going to beat this cancer. He was doing much better physically. Having survived himself, he turned all his attention to his patients. What were their needs? How could he go about making sure that those in underserved communities, who had no one looking out for their healthcare needs, would find the right doctors and the proper care? It was through the crucible of cancer that ChenMed's mission and purpose were born. The clinical model was in place before Dad ever discovered the tumor.

The service model we adopted by adding the word "love" to our values and training our people to love their patients came from Dad's experience as a patient himself.

"Chris, we have to care," he said. "We will not make our patients go through what we just went through. We must change the system."

Our experience transformed the way we as a family understood and delivered healthcare to our patients, who would no longer have to fight the system to try to get the care they needed. We would have a patient-centric medical center guiding them through the process and making sure their needs were met.

Dad survived that cancer, and he has been cancer-free ever since. As we look back at that terrifying time in the rearview mirror, we're thankful for the care he received at MD Anderson. The medical team there was used by God to heal our father. We're thankful for all the prayer warriors who faithfully prayed every day for Dad and our family, and of course, we're thankful for our loving Heavenly Father who orchestrated this all for good.

One of the great goods that came out of this experience for Dad, for our family, and for what is now ChenMed is this: every decision we make and everything we do is informed by an empathy, an understanding, a compassion for what the patients who come to us are going through. Before this happened, Dad had a great plan from a medical and physician's perspective for how to provide care for those whom other doctors and insurance companies didn't want to serve. Now his physician's plan is balanced by an understanding of what a patient experiences while seeking that care.

Dad's cancer scare was far from the only valley our family ever traversed. Mom and Dad's journey to America from Taiwan and China, and the route through poverty God led us on before we experienced any success, are other important and redemptively beautiful aspects of our story.

# CHAPTER 2

# DAD and MOM: HUMBLE BEGINNINGS

DAD WAS BORN in the city of Fuzhou (pronounced *Foo-chow*) during Mao Zedong's brutal rule. Located in south-eastern China, five hundred miles south of Shanghai, today it's a city of almost eight million people. It's located on China's largest river, the Min, close to where it empties into the South China Sea. One hundred fifty-five miles across that sea to the east is Taipei, the capital city of Taiwan.

When he was six months old, Jen-ling, our dad's Chinese name, was smuggled out of China in a fruit basket by an aunt and taken to Taipei. Dad's parents had fled the Communist regime with his older brother shortly after Dad was born.

The reason he'd been left behind? Dad was a family outcast, even as a baby. An older sister had died shortly before Dad was born, and according to one Chinese superstition, a child born in the same year that another child dies is cursed—that child "stole" the life of the dead child and will bring bad luck to the family. Throughout much of his life, Dad was verbally and physically abused by his mom, dad, and older brother. That's why Dad, and not the older brother, was forced to carry around a disabled younger brother, who eventually died at a young age.

Dad's father became the head of Taiwanese intelligence and moved the entire family to Vietnam during the war there. They lived like royalty, with abundant household help and anything an adolescent could want or imagine. Dad received an excellent education, and he learned Cantonese. He remembers that time as the golden years of his childhood. It all went away, however, when it was suspected that his father was part of a plot to assassinate a potential successor to Mao Zedong in Communist China. Authorities came down hard on our grandfather even though there was no clear evidence against him. He was arrested, along with others, and spent eight years being tortured in prison.

The family lost everything.

Back in Taiwan, Dad, as a thirteen-year-old, was forced to work to support the family. The other children were not. We believe that the family thought it was Dad, the cursed child, who'd brought this misfortune on the family. He went from being a rich diplomat's son to the lowest rung of the Taiwanese economic ladder. He often had nothing to eat and suffered from malnutrition. Dad now had to educate himself while earning minimal money as a tutor teaching other Taiwanese children.

It turns out he did a pretty good job of it. One day, two

journalists showed up at the family home, asking for Dad. His mom started beating him with a broom, screaming at him. "What did you do? I knew you were good for nothing!" she said. "You're nothing but a piece of dung!"

One of the journalists stopped her. "We're not here because your son has done anything wrong," he said. "We're here to interview him. He received the top score on the Taiwan National Entrance Exam!" This is a test that all Taiwanese high school students take, and their score determines which university they'll enter. This would be equivalent to scoring the top SAT score in America, assuming there could be only one top score!

Getting that number one score was a tremendous achievement and honor, and it proved to be another amazing turn of fortune. Because of his top score, Dad was the first student chosen and enrolled at Taiwan's most prestigious university, Taiwan National University, with a full scholarship and all expenses covered. However, his family still made him earn money to support them. Dad continued to tutor while taking a full load of classes. And that's how he met Mom.

LEE SHAO MEI, now known as Mary Chen, was born in Tainan, Taiwan, where her family had fled from Communist China a couple of years earlier. The fourth of six daughters with one brother, Mom had the responsibility of caring for her two younger sisters since both of her parents worked outside the home.

If there actually were a female warrior tribe, like the one

Wonder Woman was born into, Mom would be a part of it! These sisters were beautiful, faithful, intense, and committed to their family. They were known by their number—Sister Number One through Sister Number Six. When the family moved to Taipei, their fierce, clever mother insisted that they get a house right beside the Taiwan National University campus. She was on the lookout for the smartest husbands she could find for her six daughters. In the United States, athletic ability, looks, and wealth are the main attractions for prospective brides. In Asian culture, it's intelligence.

Grandma Lee had discovered that the top thirty students in each class all lived in one large dorm room. She sent Grandpa Lee, an electrician, to that dorm to hire tutors for their daughters. It was a brilliant plan. While none of the daughters married their own tutors, their other sisters attracted the tutors' attention. Mom's Sister Number Two married Taiwan's number two student. Sister Number Three married another student in the top thirty. Grandma Lee kept fishing in that barrel, and Mom, Sister Number Four, married Dad, Taiwan's number one student. Sister number five later married a student in the top five, who was also in Dad's class.

Not only that, but along with Dad, Sister Number Three's husband and Sister Number Five's husband would also graduate from the University of Miami School of Medicine's highly competitive program, a two-year medical program for PhD graduates. This program selected one student for every fifty PhD applicants, and the Lee sisters' husbands had completed PhDs at the University of Wisconsin, Princeton, and MIT.

Warrior tribe women, every one of them—they knew what they wanted, and they went out and got it.

MOM CAME TO FAITH as a young girl, like her mother, grandmother, and aunt, and her family attended a small Taiwanese church. She believed her life partner should share her faith, so when her younger sister's tutor, Jen-ling (aka, James Chen), fell in love with her, she took matters into her own hands and scheduled him to be baptized at her church.

Her thought was, *Let's just get it done.* Dad, however, didn't show up.

At first, she was angry. The next time she saw him, she said, "I can't believe you didn't show up!"

"I need to understand what this religion is all about before I can accept it," said Dad. "I can't get baptized just to marry you."

While it took her a while to get over being "stood up" for the baptism, she now tells what she thought about him afterward. "That told me a lot about your dad's character," said Mom. "I knew he was a good man with strong principles."

He soon learned that there was a strong group of Christians at Taiwan National University in the chemistry department. He began to attend meetings of InterVarsity Christian Fellowship on campus to learn more about what it meant to be a follower of Christ. The group included faculty members whom he admired. *These are supposed to be brilliant people*, he thought. *Why do they believe this foreign religion? There must be something to it!*

After spending four years at the Chinese Cultural College

majoring in music, Mom, who is a year older than Dad, received a scholarship to Wittenberg University in Springfield, Ohio, for a master's degree in choral conducting. Dad wanted to go to graduate school in the US as well, but he had to stay and serve, as all male Taiwanese do, in the Taiwanese military for one year. During the year that they were separated by half the globe, Dad got very serious about his faith in Christ. On Easter Sunday, he went to church. When the pastor asked if anyone would like to be baptized, Dad stepped forward and literally took the plunge. Quickly following his baptism, he wrote Mom a letter to tell her that he now shared her faith, and they could eventually get married.

On one of his visits to see Mom in Ohio, he happened to see that her visa was about to expire. Practical and in problem-solving mode, he said to her, "Let's get married now! Then you can stay in the United States."

Reflecting their no-nonsense approach and strong faith in God, within a few days, they quickly married right on campus in the Wittenberg chapel. No family and only four friends were there for the ceremony. Mom and Dad simply wore the best clothes they owned at the time—no expensive white wedding dress or rented tuxedo. Mom prepared the meal herself for their guests after the wedding, but it turned out that the food she had to prepare was spoiled. Today a bride being responsible for preparing food herself and serving her own wedding guests is unheard of. She did, however, learn a valuable lesson on food preparation, which would later come in very helpful for her as a restaurant entrepreneur.

Once they were settled in St. Louis, Mom got a job as the choral director at a Presbyterian church, but Dad discovered that job opportunities using his master's degree in chemistry were limited. A PhD in biochemistry offered more possibilities, and the University of Wisconsin in Madison had one of the top programs in the country. But rather than simply applying on paper, he traveled to Madison and started knocking on tenured professors' doors. "Could you use a hardworking, dedicated teaching assistant?" he said. "I would be very honored to have the opportunity to work with you."

World-renowned researcher Dr. Henry Lardy was impressed with Dad's credentials and desire. He said "Yes," and our parents were off to Wisconsin. While Dad began his doctoral studies, Mom completed a teaching certificate to expand her job possibilities, and they joined a Bible study with other Chinese students. Dad became president of the student group, and together they worked hard to disciple young believers in Christ and to share the good news of Christ with nonbelievers. While interest in growing as a Christ follower attracted a number of participants, the delicious meals Mom cooked for every meeting encouraged regular attendance by young, hungry students as well.

While they were in Madison, Dad's older brother came to the United States asking for help to start a restaurant. Following old family patterns, Dad felt like he owed it to him to do it. If Mom had not seen potential in his brother's restaurant idea, she and Dad never would have helped with that first restaurant. Early in their marriage, our warrior tribe mom had let his family know things were changing and Dad would not be pushed around anymore. Her deep and abiding sense of justice, combined with her strong will, empowered her to stand up against Dad's lifetime of abuse. But the response among the Chinese students to her cooking was so great that, combined with the possibility of increased income over what she was making with other jobs, she encouraged Dad to say "Yes" to his brother.

They opened The Great Wall on the second floor of a local mall. It was a small, buffet-style restaurant with nice ambience. Mom's business acumen soon emerged, and the restaurant proved extremely successful, but she became more and more wrapped up in the business and less and less available to help Dad with the Bible study. When he confronted her about where her true commitment lay, she blew it off. He told her he would pray that God would show her what she should do and where she should spend her time.

Not too long after that, a fire broke out in the mall, and her restaurant was one of the many casualties. Undeterred, Mom found a new, larger location in a dedicated building, and reopened The Great Wall. The business continued to do so well that she decided to open a third restaurant, then another with Dad's brother in Oshkosh. As Mom tells it, if you had asked anyone in the Madison Chinese community at that time who among them was the most successful businessperson, everyone would answer, "Mary Chen."

Dad continued to focus on his doctoral studies, teaching assignments, and leading the Bible study. Mom was now so consumed by her restaurant business that she had no time for the Bible study or even church on Sundays. She did find time to give birth to their first child, Chris, but soon relegated him to constant childcare because both she and Dad were so busy. She was happy doing something she loved, and she was obviously very good at it. Even though Dad appreciated the income and success Mom was experiencing, he grew more and more concerned about its impact on her spiritually and on the family. When she became pregnant with Gordon, he finally gave her an ultimatum. "Mary, if you don't give more time to the family and to the Lord, I will pray for God to take this business away!"

"But Jim!" she argued. "We are married. We are one. If my business fails, you will have no money either. And when my business is successful, I have more money to give to God!"

"God doesn't need your money, Mary," he replied. "He's much more interested in your soul. I would much rather have a wife who loves God than one who loves money!"

Mom was resistant, but she agreed to pray about it. She prayed, "Lord, if you will give me a sign, I will be happy to close the restaurants."

While all of this was going on, Dad was approaching the end of his doctoral studies. He learned of a trial program at the University of Miami's medical school in which individuals with a PhD could complete an MD program in two years, greatly increasing his range of income possibilities. He applied and was placed on the wait list.

June of that year came, and the largest blizzard on record swept through the state of Wisconsin. Chris remembers as a three-year-old the snow being so high that Dad had to lift him up on his shoulders to carry him above the drifts. But the weather changed quickly, the sun came out, and the rapidly melting snow caused massive flooding all over the state. When Mom arrived at the main restaurant, she discovered the space filled with water. A health inspector came and told her she had to shut it down. Insurance would not cover the investment they had in it.

Then another fire in the strip mall where their second restaurant was located led to significant smoke damage, leaving their second restaurant inoperable. Finally, there was no money left to run the third restaurant, so she had to give it up as well. They had to declare bankruptcy. They lost everything. Mom had gotten her sign from God, and Dad's prayer was answered.

Not knowing what would come next and within days of Gordon's birth, Dad received a call from the University of Miami's medical program.

"Have you finished your PhD?" the caller asked.

"Yes, just one week ago!" he answered.

"Well, a student just dropped out of our two-year program. Would you like to take her spot?"

Two days later, Dad was on his way to Miami. Even that great news, however, was tempered on his arrival at registration. The first thing he noticed was that there were two lines: one was for those with a doctorate who would be self-funded, the other was for those who would require financial aid. No one stood in the financial aid assistance line. Dad humbly approached that desk and gave his name. The person looked at him quizzically.

"It says on your application that you own three restaurants

and will be self-funded," she said. "That's why we accepted you! We didn't think you would need any money. Why are you asking for financial aid?"

Uncomfortable and despondent, Dad explained how they had lost their business. He thought, *At least, Lord, you let me get into medical school.* Mom and Dad learned later that it wasn't just the cream of the academic crop who got into this program, but that all of those admitted were also wealthy enough to cover the two years' expenses. It humiliated Dad to be the only person standing in the financial aid line.

When he was asked, "Why didn't you run away when you were humiliated in that line?" Dad answered, "I had hope!" He and Mom both learned to be careful what you pray for; God just might give it to you.

A COUPLE OF WEEKS later, Mom flew into Miami International Airport with the two of us—we were three years old and two weeks old. Before Dad arrived to pick us up, she had to leave us for a moment to get our luggage. She put Gordon's baby carrier on the floor and said to Chris, "You wait right here! Don't you dare move. Take care of your little brother!"

This became a common theme in our family. While Mom is one of the most caring people you will ever meet—everyone who gets to know her experiences her generosity—she is also a graduate of the "un-nurturing mothers' school" and offers "tough love." She was the exact opposite of a helicopter mom.

For example, when Chris and Stephanie were having trouble getting their first child, James, to sleep through the night, Stephanie, in her sleep-deprived state, asked Mom how she handled it. "From one to two years old, Chris would climb out of his crib and wake me up every night, wanting a bottle," Mom said. "Every night! When he turned two, just before bed, I took him to the refrigerator, opened it, and showed him where I put his bottle. 'Don't you ever wake me up again! You get your own bottle and get back in your crib.' He never woke me up again."

"You mean your two-year-old was climbing out of his crib in the middle of the night, wandering around the house, going into the refrigerator, and climbing back into his crib unsupervised, and you were okay with that?" Stephanie said.

"Yes!" Mom answered.

When Gordon turned two, Mom made him tie his own shoes.

"I don't want to do that anymore," she told him. "You do it yourself from now on."

Back at the airport in Miami, as soon as she had gathered our luggage, Mom came back. She remembers three-year-old Chris standing in the exact spot where she had left us, unsmiling, like a guard dog protecting his little brother.

When we finally got outside and met Dad, who had come to pick us up, Mom asked him where we were going to spend the night.

"Well, I have an appointment for us to see about getting an apartment," he said.

"An apartment!" she protested. "They will ask for the first month's rent, last month's rent, and a one-month security deposit. I only have seven hundred dollars that my sister loaned me. We can't rent an apartment. Is there anyone you can ask to let us stay tonight?"

Thankfully, one of Dad's classmates in medical school had offered to put us up for a couple of nights while we got settled. Then, through the church, we learned of a woman from Taiwan who was going back home for a few months. We were able to stay in that apartment for three months with her husband, who remained in Miami. Over the next couple of years, we moved seven times. Mom calls it "living in temporary housing." We call it being homeless, bouncing from one friend's place to another, sleeping on couches, floor mats, or whatever might be available for a growing family of four.

Mom's experience losing three restaurants and having to declare bankruptcy, along with the years of dependency on help from others, taught her some valuable lessons, which she taught us: always have money in reserve, be financially conservative, and have an emergency fund.

We can only imagine the pressure Dad and Mom were under. It would be difficult enough to complete a medical degree in two years—many fail to do it in the standard four. They had no money, two very young children, and no place to call home. Academic pressure. Financial pressure. Family pressure. Our admiration and appreciation for our parents never ceases to grow.

We asked Dad how he handled those years. His answer? "God's power—it was the only way I could sustain the focus, the energy, and the faith I needed to get through those two years."

NEVER ONE TO SIT back and accept bad circumstances, Mom scoured the paper for different work and living conditions that could improve our family's situation. She found an answer for both in one ad. A family was looking for a housekeeper and live-in nanny for their child, who was a few months older than Gordon. Mom got the job, and we were all allowed to move into the duplex apartment they owned within walking distance of Dad's classes. This job was an answer to the prayer she had prayed while pregnant with Gordon: "Lord, I haven't been around much while Chris was growing up. Please give me a job where I can be present for my second child."

Mom's new boss was a pediatrician who became concerned about Gordon's low weight. She contacted a formula manufacturer and got free formula for him. At the same time, Mom learned that we qualified for food stamps. "When I thought about all the money I paid in taxes from my restaurants, I was OK with getting help when my family needed it," says Mom.

With food stamps for four people plus free formula for Gordon, we ate very, very well for a while. Gordon went from malnourished to overweight in a hurry. Perhaps that's why he has a voracious appetite to this day!

When the job with the pediatrician and her family ended, Mom got a job at The Debbie School, an organization run by the University of Miami's School of Pediatric Medicine that serves children with disabilities. She told the people at the Medicaid and health services office that we didn't need food stamps anymore.

"I just got a job. I don't think I qualify for food stamps anymore," she said.

"How much are you making?" the person asked. "Are you sure you want me to cancel your food stamps?"

"I'm sure. Absolutely. If I don't qualify, I shouldn't get them."

The woman at the desk looked up at Mom.

"I've been working here for more than twenty years," she said. "No one ever came in to tell me they didn't want the food stamps anymore. You're the first. Are you absolutely sure?"

"Yes," said Mom. "Give the money to someone else who needs it."

IN HER TWO POSITIONS at The Debbie School, working first with toddlers and then preschoolers, Mom was allowed to bring Gordon with her to class since he was the same age as the students she served. God continued to answer Mom's prayer to be with her second child as he grew. When Gordon started kindergarten, however, Mom got a job teaching at a different public school. While there, she learned something that none of us have forgotten.

Mom served as a tutor to one of the fifth-grade teachers at that public school. Yes, *the teacher*. She could not pass the fifth-grade math she was supposed to be teaching. If a teacher herself cannot do the work, how can she possibly help fifth graders learn and go on to success? We later discovered that Mom's experience with the fifth-grade teacher was not unique. Many teachers in certain school districts do not have the skills and resources they need to adequately teach their classes.

DAD FINISHED his two years of study at the University of Miami School of Medicine and began his residency at Jackson Memorial Hospital, the same institution his school had used for instruction. During his residency, he was expected to work a minimum of one hundred hours a week. Those were the days before work hour restrictions were put in place for residents. Mom was also working very long hours at the public school. The two of us, from the time that Gordon was four until Chris was nine, were often left at home alone.

When questioned about having to leave us alone, Mom says, "By God's mercy and grace, we got through it. It was a different time."

During those first years in Miami, we had a Volkswagen Beetle that was close to twenty years old. Those old Beetles had open slats in the back metal cover over the rear engine. The starter was located just inside those slats, and every time it rained, the starter would get wet and couldn't ignite the engine. Not only that, but we were in South Florida, where it rains every day.

And so, when it was time for Mom to take us to school and go to work herself each day, she would sit in the driver's seat, and six-year-old Chris would be behind the Beetle, pushing her off. She would pop the clutch, get the car started, and then drive back around the block to pick up Chris. Once we got it started, we couldn't turn the car off until we reached our final destination. Someone eventually put some cardboard inside the metal cover to block rain from getting on the starter, and that helped for a while. One time, another driver was honking their horn at our mom, yelling and screaming frantically, and she discovered that her engine had caught fire! Thankfully we were protected from that fire and eventually replaced the Beetle with an ancient, used Cadillac, which turned out to be even less reliable than the Volkswagen.

When Dad started his residency, we moved into a seventeenth-floor apartment in Jackson Towers, an apartment building for the residents in his program. One of the first improvements we noticed, which was only apparent to two young boys, was that the roaches were smaller there than at some of the other places we lived. Those "roaches," known as palmetto bugs in the Southeast, are huge, prehistoric trauma-inducing creatures that are two inches long with wings that allow them to fly onto you while you're sleeping in bed at night.

There was a pool on the roof of Jackson Towers, and the two of us would venture up from our apartment to ride our bicycles around the pool. One day Gordon, who was just learning to ride his bike, became quite unsteady trying to negotiate the narrow space between the outer wall and the edge of the pool. Chris noticed his younger brother was no longer right behind him. He looked around and saw Gordon entangled in his bike at the bottom of the pool.

*That doesn't look good*, he thought. Since Gordon was

Chris's responsibility and there was no one else around, his only choice was to dive in. After a brief struggle to free Gordon's leg from the frame of his bike, the two of us headed back down to our apartment, soaking wet in the elevator.

By this time, we were both learning to swim. Dad taught Chris by showing him a dog in the water. "Just do what the dog is doing!" he said.

Chris copied the dog's paddling motion, and that's how he learned to swim.

During the summers before the incident on the roof of Jackson Towers, Mom would take us to Venetian Pool, a public swimming complex not too far from where we lived. She would drop us off in the morning, give Chris two dollars for our admission and lunch, and tell us she would be back to pick us up that afternoon. Chris was in charge for the day.

It was around this time that someone at the church told Mom that she was a horrible mother. We both disagree. All you have to do is consider how her sons turned out and the love and devotion to one another we share as a family. Sure, we know she was tough. If we wanted comforting when we were little, we would go to Dad, not Mom. She would tell us to just get over whatever the problem was. From Dad, we received guidance and a worldview—how to think, what it means to be men of faith, and how to treat others with a philosophy of care.

Gordon remembers standing with Dad at a vending machine to get a soda. He put his money in, and two cans came out. Gordon was excited about getting the extra soda. But Dad made him leave one of them, because we hadn't paid for the second one.

"What are you talking about? We got two sodas!" Gordon tried to argue.

Dad would have none of it. He taught us to go by the book in doing the right thing, no matter how easy it might be to do otherwise.

What we learned from Mom was independence, the value of hard work, perseverance, and what it means to be a leader. "You're in charge now. Go figure it out!" she would say.

When Gordon was around five, Mom bought him a toy. She warned him that if he didn't play with it, she would make him return it. After several days, she found the toy unused, lying around the apartment. She made Gordon get in the car, drove him to the store, and told him to go in and get the money back. Gordon had to make several trips back and forth for advice from Mom, who sternly waited in the car. At first the salesperson wouldn't allow him to return it.

"Go back in there!" Mom said.

"But they asked me, 'Where's your mom?'" he said.

"Tell them I'm in the car. Now go back in!"

Someone in the store finally allowed Gordon to return it and gave him the refund. It would have been much easier for Mom to have returned it herself. But to her, it was more important in that situation for her son to learn a lesson. She has often told us when talking about the way we raise our own children: "It's easier to do it for them. It's much harder to teach. But it's never too early for them to learn how to do things on their own."

Neither of us would be the men—the husbands, the fathers, the doctors—we are if Mom or Dad had treated us any differently. We could never ask for better parents. We had the best!

# CHAPTER 3

# TIGER PARENTING 2.0

OUR PARENTS had very strong opinions on how to raise children. As Chris and Stephanie started having their own, Chris asked Dad for advice.

"Your job is guidance and philosophy," he said. "Never tell your children to do something, or not to do something, without telling them why. You say, 'This is what I want you to do, and this is why,' or, 'Do not ever do this, and here is why. . . .'"

When Dad mentions philosophy, he means a worldview. And after studying it diligently, the worldview he came to hold for himself and then communicated to us was one based on his understanding of the Bible. His worldview is not at the ten-thousand-foot level or even the one-hundred-thousand-foot level. It's from a million-plus-mile level and beyond.

"What is God's view on this?" he would ask. "I trained you, and I hope you will train your children to take this view. What is God's purpose for creation? What is God's purpose for *you*?"

Remember Dad's approach to becoming a man of faith? He took his time to study, and he wanted to understand for himself why highly intelligent men and women embrace Christianity. For him and now for us, it is a cogent, well-thought-out, and reasoned acceptance of this faith, grounded in enormous amounts of logic. For Dad, his philosophy came from a biblical worldview, and his guidance always began with the "why" of what he was asking of us.

If you ask Mom how to raise children, she will tell you that it's all about accountability. She is the tiger mom of tiger moms, and she's ruthless regarding expectations. Chris and Stephanie asked her the same question they asked Dad about raising children. Her answer?

"It is not possible for you to set high enough expectations," she said.

"Is there anything else?" Chris asked.

"No. There is nothing else. You cannot set high enough expectations."

Chris remembers Mom sitting him down for a talk when he was still quite young. "Chris," she said. "We are going to push you hard. Very hard. Get used to it. That is the way it is going to be. You do not have a say in this." With Mom, we both knew not to argue. She went on. "As I have told you many times, you are responsible for Gordon," she said. "If Gordon fails, it's on you. He is your responsibility. And if he succeeds, you've done your job. It is to your credit."

Chris's task, which he always knew, was to invest in Gordon. For Gordon, the approach was slightly different. His task was to take what he learned from Chris and blow it out of the water, to take it to the next level. It was a failure of the system if either of those two things did not occur.

There's a Chinese saying—"One to grow, one to maintain, one to lose." With an accumulation of five thousand years of wisdom in that culture, much truth about human nature can be learned from it. This saying speaks to what happens in too many families. One generation will grow something, the next merely maintains what the previous one grew, and the next one loses what they had. Our parents were intentional in seeing to it that ours would not be one of those families.

"You are acting like one of those generations!" they'd lecture when we were being punished.

We knew exactly what they meant. Mom and Dad did everything they could to make sure that we would not be the generation that merely maintains, or even worse, *loses*, what they as the previous generation had worked so hard to grow. And so they pushed both of us hard—Chris to be his very best and to invest all of his best into his younger brother, and for Gordon never to be satisfied with anything less than surpassing Chris.

"Why is Gordon so competitive?" asked Stephanie, soon after she and Chris were married.

Chris looked at her like he didn't understand.

"What do you mean? He's not competitive," he replied.

"Of course he is! Why else would he constantly be asking how you're doing, and then always have to one-up you?"

She had hit on something that was ingrained in us. Gordon wasn't competing with Chris. He was simply fulfilling his purpose, completing the plan. Around that same time, Chris ran his fastest time in a 5K race: 19:01. He called Gordon and asked him when he would be running his next 5K.

"Three months," he said.

"Okay," said Chris. "Here's what I did to train, and here's what I got. Go do this, this, and this. You know the recipe. Now go."

Gordon's time three months later? 18:59.

When Gordon started medical school, before he began each semester, he would question Chris.

"What did you do to study for this class?"

"I read these three books," said Chris. "Ignore that, that, and that. Just read those three at least once."

"What did you get?" Gordon would ask.

"I got a ninety-five. Now you know what's expected, right, Gordon?"

At the end of the semester, Gordon's grade came in—ninety-seven. It happened every time.

As YOU MAY have picked up by now, we spent a lot of time together, just the two of us, during those first years in South Florida. Dad was consumed with school and then residency, while Mom scrambled to find work and pay bills. The episode at the airport when we arrived in Miami, with the three-year-old being tasked to watch over the two-week-old baby, became our way of life. Our most common meals were Chef Boyardee out of a can or a burger at Hardee's, which was just down the street from Jackson Towers.

That Hardee's became the location for some of our earliest competitions. Chris had the money to pay for our food. Once we sat down to eat, he would suggest a race to see who could finish his burger the fastest. With his three-year age advantage and bigger size, Chris would get down to his last bite much faster than Gordon, but then stop. Pointing out to Gordon how close he was to winning, Chris encouraged his much younger brother to hurry. He even offered his help.

"Do you want me to help you eat yours so you can catch up?" he asked.

Unsuspecting of what was at play, Gordon would nod in the affirmative. With his older brother's help, Gordon would win our burger-eating competition. But he lost much of his burger in the process.

Having an older sibling responsible for a younger one was not unique to our immediate family. We learned later that this was exactly how Mom was raised. Number One Sister was given the responsibility for Number Two, Number Two for Number Three, and right on down the line through Number Six. Not only that, but each successive sister was expected to outachieve the previous one because of the advantage she had been given of having her older sister's help and modeling. For example, Number Two Sister was able to attend college in the

United States and did very well because of the hard work and financial sacrifices Number One had made for her.

For us, it meant that those early years were rather happy-go-lucky for Gordon, other than rarely getting to finish a whole burger. He felt secure and protected, never deprived, because Chris was always there to take care of him. Chris, however, felt abandoned, especially by Dad. Chris's strong, alpha male personality led him to become angry and rebellious toward Dad. *Who is this other male who shows up occasionally and wants to be in charge?* It didn't sit well with him. Chris was always getting in trouble, and just as he had during the good times, he made sure to take Gordon along with him into trouble as well.

One way we got into trouble was what led us to believe that Dad had superpowers. With Mom and Dad gone so much and us at home together unsupervised, we watched a lot of TV. Once Dad finished his residency and started making money, we moved to a nice house in Sky Lake, a predominantly Jewish neighborhood in North Miami Beach. Our parents had one of those beds with a remote that allowed you to raise and lower the back. We would climb up on that bed and watch the Cartoon Network and all the popular shows of the 1980s for hours. A problem arose for us, however, because one of the rules of the house was a limit of one hour of TV per day. But we figured—how could they know if they were gone all day? Chris insisted that it was OK for us to ignore the one-hour rule.

But Dad's superpowers enabled him to bust us. When we heard them drive up at night, we would quickly turn off the TV and pick up a book, feigning innocence. With fear and trembling, however, we watched Dad come in, go behind the TV for a moment, and then call us out. (We figured out later that he was feeling to see if the back of the TV was hot—if it was, he knew we were still watching just as they arrived home.) In Chinese tradition—and speaking in Chinese—he would demand that we kneel down in front of him to take our punishment. Then we would get a very stern lecture.

That could have been the extent of it if only Chris would have let it. But he wouldn't. He would stand up and argue with Dad. Gordon remembers thinking—*Come on, dude! Let it go! Just do the time and it's over!*

But, no. Chris would stand and scream at Dad even louder. Since we had committed the crime together, we had to suffer the consequences together. We frequently suffered two or three times the punishment our joint offense deserved.

It shouldn't be a surprise that two headstrong brothers didn't always agree. When we had conflicts with each other, we couldn't run to Mom or Dad to help us settle them. "When we die, you will only have each other," they said, and then, to Chris, "You must take care of your brother."

We had lots of fights. When we were around ages eight and eleven, Chris had Gordon's hair in his hand, and Gordon had Chris's arm in his teeth.

"You let go!" Chris said.

"No, *you* let go!"

"*You* let go!"

"No, *you* let go!"

You get the idea. This could go on for quite a while.

We would always make up, especially as it got close to meal-time. We both loved to eat, and we would never allow anything to get in the way of doing that.

Once, Mom caught us eating doughnuts when we weren't supposed to. "OK, you want to eat doughnuts?" she said. "Eat doughnuts! Eat every single one, right now!" Chris thought, *Cool!*

Gordon wasn't so sure it was a good idea, and he was right, at least for him. After one too many, his all came back up.

BEFORE WE MOVED to Sky Lake, we lived in Liberty City, Florida, one of Miami's roughest neighborhoods. We were poor like everyone around us, but we stood out as different—two Chinese boys in a sea of Black and Hispanic people.

Someone once asked, "Why is Gordon so sophisticated and Chris is such a thug?"

What people often didn't see and know about Chris was his artistic, creative side. Mom sometimes got frustrated that Chris didn't further develop his musical gift. As an adolescent, he received superior ratings on his piano performances. But shortly after puberty, he rebelled and gave up his keyboard training.

Chris became more of a barbarian on the streets of Liberty City. Not only did he have to fight his own battles, but he had the responsibility of protecting and taking care of Gordon as well. We've come to realize something about human nature that was true in the streets of Liberty City. It's true in the boardrooms of major corporations. And it's true in far too many of our homes. Until we submit ourselves to the redeeming work God desires to do through us, which is to form and shape the character qualities he created us to have, we at some point revert to our basest selves. Chris learned about human nature and developed lots of street smarts during those years in Liberty City. He learned how people think at a deep, fundamental level. Whether it's in gangs or prison populations or a boys' dorm at a boarding school, people are no different. At their core, the battles between humans are the same. We may wear different clothes, use different weapons, and play with different toys, but people are always looking to oppress other people. It's the unfortunate nature of original sin, which has infected us all and affects how we relate to one another.

When Dad started making money, Chris struggled with the transition to a much wealthier neighborhood and lifestyle. He had learned how to survive and work the system in a lower-income life. This situation, by the way, helps explain one of the major differences between us. Chris processes information intuitively—he inherited the creative, right-brain thinking from Mom, with her master's degree in choral and orchestral conducting. With that intuition comes more emotion and spontaneity. He prefers to step back, take in the big picture, and then work his way down to the finer points while learning how the system works.

When he was correcting Chris on how he was dealing with something, Dad would often say, "Chris, Chris, Chris. Don't right-brain this!"

Gordon, on the other hand, thinks methodically from

the bottom up. He inherited that measured, process-oriented way of thinking from Dad. He's more levelheaded and reasonable, able to fit smoothly into an established plan and then excel in it.

In this new, very different environment, surrounded by a predominantly affluent Jewish community, Chris didn't know how to interact or function. He was quickly ostracized. What does a ten- or eleven-year-old do when he doesn't know the brand names of jeans, much less which ones he should be wearing? Chris recalls being invited to a bar mitzvah and showing up without a suit. He didn't know there was such a thing! The kids, like always, were ruthless.

Gordon had a much easier transition. He had been one step removed from the lessons of the streets, and he soon developed friendships in our new school and neighborhood. As the only two Asian kids, we both took tennis lessons at the Jewish Community Center (JCC), which was within walking distance of our home. When Chris was eleven and Gordon eight, we were at the JCC when a couple of older boys stopped us. Gordon was allowed to pass, but one of the teenagers punched Chris in the face. And it was *on*. Rarely did a day go by that Chris wasn't in a fight. He was angry, he had a short fuse, and he had a lot of passion.

We were always big for our ages, a couple of jocks. We didn't fit in at school or at our Chinese Baptist Church. Our public schools, Highland Oaks Elementary and Highland Oaks Junior High, were 80 percent upper-income Jewish and 20 percent underprivileged Black and Hispanic, with a few poorer

White kids thrown in. That entire 20 percent was bused in to increase diversity at the school.

Gordon, being more even-keeled and mellow, was able to adapt and fit in with the majority group. Most of the friends he made were Jewish. You get one guess as to which group Chris quickly identified with. If you said the jocks, you are correct.

WHEN CHRIS AND STEPHANIE'S son James was around eight years old, Chris came home from work one day to a troubled household. Stephanie greeted him at the door.

"We've had a very rough day today, Chris," she started. "James was bullied at school."

Immediately Chris reverted to his teenaged self. All that anger, passion, and sense of justice rose up inside him.

"What?" Chris said. "I hate bullies! Were they bigger kids?"

"Yeah, they were bigger kids."

Chris went to James's room to hear the whole story.

"Hey, son, Mom told me what happened today," he started.

"Yeah, these kids were making fun of me," James said.

"I know. That really stinks," said Chris. "I was the only Chinese kid in my grade at my school. I got picked on nonstop. So what happened next?"

"Well, they kept picking on me," said James.

"Yeah, yeah. But then—did they punch you in the face?"

"No, they were just making fun of me."

"Come on, son," Chris said. "You can tell me. I'm your dad. What else did they do? Did they jump you in the bathroom?"

"No."

"Did they gut punch you when no one was looking?"

"No."

"But they pushed you into the lockers, right?"

"No, Dad," said James. "They just picked on me. Those big kids made fun of me."

Chris went back down to Stephanie.

"Steph, I was about to go to town on some parents because of what their kids did to our son," he said. "And listen, I get it. It's never good to be made fun of. Nobody likes it. But what happened to James at school today is not what I call bullying. I got jumped in the bathroom, kicked in the hall, and punched in the face and the gut. *That* is bullying!"

Of course, the culture has changed dramatically since we were kids. Today what James experienced is the definition of bullying. But back when we were growing up, Chris's temperament and size discouraged anyone from messing with Chris Chen's younger brother.

We're often asked if we had racial taunts or slurs hurled at us. The answer is "Yes." But we didn't really identify as Chinese because our parents had such a bad experience with communism in China. We never fit in at our Chinese church because we were so big, especially compared to all the other Chinese kids. We would get stares as if we were aliens. In fact, neither of our parents is especially big. As kids, we fantasized that for Dad's doctoral thesis in bioengineering, he had run some experiments with growth hormones and we were his dissertation: "Look what I did! I can make big Chinese boys!"

So yes, we did have racial taunts and slurs thrown at us. Chris's nickname in school was Chino, and Gordon inherited that name after Chris graduated. But we never paid any attention to it. Neither of us ever focused on being a victim; we were always too busy going after the prize! We put every effort into attacking life, using all the vigor we had to pursue whatever goal was immediately in front of us. Being called a name would never stop us or slow us down. Our response? *Whatever.*

A racial taunt or slur was never an excuse or a defense mechanism that either one of us would allow ourselves to use.

For Chris, being a big, strong Chinese kid meant almost every testosterone-raging alpha male between the ages of ten and seventeen put a target on his back. By his senior year in high school, at six foot four or five and two hundred twenty pounds, there weren't many people who wanted to mess with him. But in the years leading up to that, there were plenty.

During those early years, Chris didn't remain isolated as the lone Chinese kid. He did what others did when ganged up on—he found others who would fight with him. Chris entered a world of *us versus them*—the goal was to establish dominance, with one group more powerful and threatening than the other. If you discovered your group wasn't strong enough, then you went out and recruited more members.

At thirteen, not only did Chris learn to drive his sixteen-year-old friend's Pontiac Grand Prix, but he was well on his way to being in a gang, one of many on the streets of Liberty City.

The turning point came when he was halfway through ninth grade. Chris and his gang were meeting a rival gang for a big fight. He left the affluent area of North Miami Beach where we lived, on the east side of I-95, and crossed over to the California Club area on the much rougher, violent west side. Everyone showed up with their blunt weapons—sticks and baseball bats. They hadn't graduated to guns and knives yet. Those would come later when they finished their training and became members of the Latin Kings.

Things changed that day, however, when a busload of cops showed up. The policemen started taking names, registering everyone at the scene. For two hours, Chris was yelled at, grilled, and experienced every scare tactic the police could employ to discourage gang participation. For Chris, it worked. He remembers being plenty scared that day. And he began to think about where he would wind up if he continued down that same path.

Mom and Dad never knew about that event. But they did see the direction Chris was headed in and the friends he was hanging out with, and they were starting to get concerned. They knew they needed to step in and do something different if they wanted to save their oldest son.

PINE CREST SCHOOL in Fort Lauderdale was established in 1934. According to Wikipedia, in 2012 the *Washington Post* ranked it second in their index of private schools in the United States. Well known for its academic rigor and athletic discipline, when Mom and Dad started looking for ways to solve the problem of Chris, their solution was a thirty-minute car ride up I-95 from Sky Lake.

Gordon cried when he learned his constant companion and mentor for the entire thirteen years of his life was being sent away. Chris's first response when he got the news that starting in tenth grade they were sending him to boarding school, was what you might expect. He fought it and fought it, like he did almost everything else, until he arrived on the Pine Crest campus for his interview. His reaction?

"Oh, my gosh! This is a *school?*"

Prior to Pine Crest, Chris had always been an excellent student—his grades were never the problem. As a junior high student, he was taking chemistry at North Miami Beach High. As long as he made good grades, Mom and Dad had pretty much left him alone until they realized trouble was brewing in the ninth grade. With his academic record in the public schools' gifted programs—always getting straight As in accelerated classes—and with recommendations from several teachers in hand, Chris got through the interview and was accepted as a boarding student.

Not all of Pine Crest's students at the time were boarders. In fact, only 10 percent were. If we had lived just ten blocks farther north, Chris could have been a day student like the other ninety percent. Instead, he was assigned to the boys' dorm, which housed jocks—great athletes recruited by the private school to improve their excellent sports program—or misfits—kids whose wealthy parents didn't want to deal with them on a daily basis.

The day students were basically the same as the students at North Miami High except their families were two to three times wealthier. Among the boarders, some of the athletes went on to compete in the Olympics. There were two professional swimmers from Greece in his dorm. The prime minister of Switzerland's son was also a "dormie," as the boarders called themselves.

During his first fall, Chris played on the football team. Other than tennis at the JCC, it was his first organized team sport. With his size and strength, he quickly found his positions on the offensive and defensive lines. When football season ended, the wrestling coaches saw his size and strength and recruited him for that team. As with football, he not only had a natural gift for it but the work ethic and self-motivation to succeed.

Many of the athletes came from dysfunctional homes. For most, someone with wealth—an alum or a parent of an alum—paid their tuition. They were a self-disciplined, ethnically diverse, rough, and angry group, which imposed its own strict hierarchical order with an iron hand. It was like a prison culture.

Chris quickly learned that the coaches of the athletic teams were the "prison guards." They either served as the dorm parents, living in the dorms, or they lived close by on campus. Every minute of the day was accounted for, with check-ins happening twice a day. Athletes were up at 5:30 a.m., training until 7:30. Then they showered, had room inspection (we had to make our beds every day), and did schoolwork until

2:30 p.m. After school, they lifted weights until 4:00 p.m., had football or wrestling practice from 4:00 until 6:30 p.m., and then went to dinner. The first check-in was at 7:45 p.m.—they had to be showered and ready for study hall, which lasted from 7:45 until 9:35 p.m. One of the senior student proctors would check on each student (there were sixty-four boy dormies at the time), making sure all were in their rooms studying. Then from 9:35 until 10:15 p.m., they had "free time."

Some learned they could run across campus to the girls' dorm, which was about three-fourths of a mile away, during that free time. But God help the dormie who wasn't back for that 10:15 p.m. check-in! The doors were locked at 10:15 sharp, and there were serious consequences if you weren't inside before the lockdown. As a sophomore that first year, Chris's lights-out curfew was 10:45. But knowing he had to be up at 5:30 the next morning to do it all again, it wasn't such a hard rule to follow.

While public school had been a breeze academically—just showing up for class and getting that A, even in Advanced Placement courses—Pine Crest proved to be as hard as medical school for Chris. The same discipline required for athletic training—four hours a day during football season and five to six hours a day for wrestling—was necessary in the classroom and study hall as well. He was pushed to the limits of his abilities physically and mentally. As a result, he grew as an athlete and a student.

The rigorous routine demanded by Pine Crest during the week was counterbalanced by our parents every weekend.

Mom and Dad were so smart! They made coming home like a vacation at a Four Seasons resort. They renovated the house during his first year away, making Chris's bedroom much bigger. Instead of sleeping like he did in the dorm on a plastic bunk bed with an egg crate mattress topper to try to make it more comfortable, he now had a king-sized bed for his growing body. Instead of an always dirty, open hallway with rows of nozzles on the tile walls called a shower facility, Chris now had his own deluxe bathroom. Instead of stepping out onto hard, cold linoleum when he got out of bed in the morning, his feet were greeted by plush, soft carpeting. And rather than having to rush to wolf down cafeteria food for every meal, there was a housekeeper in the kitchen early in the morning, filling the house with the aromas of hot, cooked, leisurely enjoyed breakfasts. Instead of always looking over his shoulder, watching out for those older, stronger athletes, our weekends were spent going out as a family to restaurants, to the movies, or back home to watch TV.

Going home was like dying and going to heaven. Think of it—a teenager excited to be at home on the weekend! Chris's relationship with Dad, which had been so difficult and fraught with fights, completely shifted. The difference between life in the dorm and life at home was stark. Chris came to appreciate how awesome our parents are.

"I'm not a fool," he says. "I knew where I had it great!"

OF COURSE, Gordon understood that where Chris went, he was likely soon to follow, so he wasn't surprised by Mom and

Dad's decision to send him to Pine Crest. At thirteen years old, Gordon started eighth grade there the next year. Chris had learned the ropes and, entering his junior year at around two hundred pounds of muscle on a six-foot-three frame, no underclassman dormie, much less a day student, was going to pick on his kid brother.

Like Chris, Gordon's experience playing football prior to arriving at Pine Crest had been pickup games in the park. He was always the tall, goofy Chinese kid, the minority among minorities.

In one game, the fastest kid on the field had the ball on offense, and Gordon was able to run him down.

"Oh, no! Chino can *move!*" the other kids shouted.

Once he arrived at Pine Crest, Gordon followed in Chris's footsteps, playing on both the offensive and defensive lines on the football team in the fall and competing as a member of the wrestling team in the winter. Playing tackle football, he became well known and respected for his ability to use his size and run over people. But as an eighth grader on the varsity team, his first time ever wrestling, he only won one match the entire season. The next year as a freshman, having gone through puberty and with his strength catching up to the size of his body, it was the reverse—Gordon won almost every match.

"After that first year, Chris served as my coach and training partner," Gordon says. "I grew in my skill level, thanks to my big brother, even as my body grew."

The two of us were the biggest members of the wrestling team that season, and we both got first place in the first tournament of the year.

Gordon had no problem adjusting to academics at Pine Crest in math or science, but English was much more difficult for him. Neither of our parents ever read to us. Our grammar was awful, and we had to do remedial work in English and grammar during the summer. The biggest difficulties for Gordon that first year, however, were adjusting to being away from home, having a roommate, and meeting the new expectations of school, sports, and dorm life as a thirteen-year-old adolescent.

AROUND THE SAME time, we started going on family skiing trips to Colorado. It was a popular family thing to do at Pine Crest. On one of those early trips, during Chris's junior year, Dad called him over early in the morning.

"You and I need to have a talk," said Dad. "Sit down. You're not going skiing today."

Shocked and rather upset, Chris asked, "Why not?"

"You don't seem very focused," Dad said. "I'm watching you, and I see you're having a lot of fun. You don't look like someone in their junior year of high school."

"What?!" Chris started to argue. "We're on vacation!"

"No, Mom and I are on vacation," Dad calmly replied. "We just bring you along. You need to prepare for war. When you're out there, it's a war. This world can be cruel and ruthless. You must be ready to compete in this ruthless world. You don't know what it feels like not to be able to feed your family."

Dad's plan from the time we were little was for both of us to go through the University of Miami's six-year medical school program and work with him in his medical practice.

While Chris was finishing up his senior year at Pine Crest, Dad felt Gordon wasn't taking school as seriously as he should. One weekend, they had a talk about it.

"Gordon, you're just as smart as your brother," Dad started. "You know, you're failing if you don't accomplish at least what your brother does. And you're not using the gifts God has given you if you don't surpass him! You have every advantage, having him as your brother."

Gordon heard Dad. But it wasn't until Chris was accepted into Miami's very competitive six-year medical school program that he knew he had to step it up. That's when Gordon took the TV out of his room at home so that he wouldn't have that distraction over weekends and during the summer.

"My competition with Chris wasn't just so I could say I beat him—it was because I knew there was no excuse I could offer Mom and Dad if I didn't," Gordon says.

OUR COMPETITION even extended to the football field, weight room, and wrestling mats. For two teenagers growing up, working out allowed us to release our frustrations and energy in a safe and constructive way. In those first couple of years at Pine Crest, Gordon was uncoordinated, but because of his size, he was good at running into and over people. When Gordon was in the ninth grade, he made the varsity football team, and we were put on opposite ends of the defensive line. As a senior, Chris was now six foot four and weighed 225 pounds. Gordon was almost as tall but only weighed one seventy-five as a freshman. To confuse the opposition, we would sometimes switch the side of the line we were on. All they knew was that one of us hit a lot harder than the other!

They saw one of us six years in a row in the state wrestling tournament, and by the time Chris had graduated, Gordon was in the same weight classification that Chris had been in. People thought, "Boy, that big Chinese kid must be really stupid. He never graduates!"

CHAPTER 4

# NOURISH, BUILD, EXCEED, REPEAT

FROM THE TIME we were fifteen and twelve years old, each summer our family went on a youth mission trip to Nicaragua with our church. The summer after our sophomore year in high school and second year at UM, Gordon was one of about seventy high schoolers, Chris was among the college-aged counselors, and Mom and Dad were there for medical support.

It's extremely hot in the summer in that tropical climate, and that year a fainting epidemic broke out among the high school girls. As two big, strong, male-protective types, we would pick the girls up and carry them, bridal-style, to Dad for medical treatment. We were too thickheaded to realize, as Mom and Dad did, that the girls were hyperventilating and causing themselves to faint—they all wanted this "romanticized" treatment.

A young girl named Stephanie was on that trip. Just as we were carrying a steady stream of girls with "the vapors" to Dad, Stephanie came in, bringing him some supplies.

"I don't know what's going on with all these girls and their issues," she said, "but they need to learn to suck it up!"

Dad looked at her, and then with his eyebrows raised, he looked at Mom. After Stephanie left the room, they talked.

"She's pretty tough. Who are her parents?" asked Dad.

"Glenn and Reta," Mom replied.

"Oh! OK. Tough missionary girl. Good parents."

At that point, the fate of one of us was sealed. Now the question—which one of their sons would marry this tough missionary girl? They observed Stephanie the rest of that trip. Even though she was closer to Gordon in age, they made their decision.

"Mary, you need to make this happen," Dad told her. "This is the girl for Chris."

Once Dad gives Mom a mission, it becomes not a question of *if* but *how soon* she accomplishes it. As Mom likes to put it, Dad makes the snowballs and he tells her where to throw them. Back in Florida, without consulting Chris or Stephanie, Mom talked with Stephanie's mother. Then she started in on Chris. We've learned it's one of the laws of nature, like gravity. Mom will wear you down. She doesn't lose. And we're both glad she doesn't! Mom called Chris every day at seven in the morning.

"Have you called Stephanie and asked her out yet?"

Chris's roommate at UM, Jason Lane, was a year older

than Chris and his "older brother" in their fraternity. Jason wasn't an early riser, and the ringing phone would wake him up. Finally, he'd had enough. "Would you please call the girl and ask her out so your mom will quit calling?" said Jason.

Three years later, when Stephanie was nineteen and Chris was twenty-three, they got married. Stephanie has proven time and time again to be the person Chris can count on when things get tough. She has one of those "I'll-run-into-the-fire-rather-than-away-from-it" personalities. When Chris had a faith crisis, she found the church for them that helped him get back on course. When Dad received his cancer diagnosis, she traveled to South Florida before Chris did to make sure the family was OK. She took the year off from law school so that she could go with Dad to Houston for treatments. Dad and Mom definitely got that one right.

By his sophomore year at Pine Crest, Gordon weighed just under 190 pounds and was the largest wrestler on the team. As a result, he had no one to practice against. That's when Chris stepped it up. For the three years that Gordon was still in high school and Chris was in the University of Miami's six-year medical school program, he drove an hour each way, every day during wrestling season, to train with Gordon from 4:00 to 6:30 p.m. Chris had made it to the state tournament all three years of his high school wrestling career, but he never placed. He considered it his responsibility to make sure Gordon did at least as well, if not better.

That first year, Gordon got fourth place in the state finals.

His junior year, he won the county tournament, districts, and regionals, and was undefeated going into the state finals. Unfortunately, he was injured during the semifinals match against the eventual state champion. Gordon finished the match with a torn MCL in his knee and lost on points. As a senior, he was also undefeated going into the state semifinals and faced the returning two-time state champion. It was probably the most-anticipated match of the tournament. Despite an early takedown and multiple lead changes, Gordon eventually lost by one point. That loss was a crushing emotional defeat for both of us—we still play that match over and over in our heads. Gordon finished 31-1 that year, placing third in the state.

Chris invested all that time into Gordon while completing his undergraduate college degree in two years and his first year of medical school. He made it through the first two years okay, but the first year of medical school? Not so much. In fact, he almost flunked out. He passed histology, the study of the microscopic structure of tissues, by one point, with a sixty-six. To this day he says, "Please don't ever show me a slide!"

At first, Gordon was a bit leery of Chris's motives for coming every day during the week to coach and train with him for wrestling. He remembered what had happened with his Hardee's hamburgers. Gordon wondered why Chris would devote twenty-plus hours a week to him, risking his own academic performance and career. At first, he didn't understand that Chris had been taught from a young age that Gordon's success was his responsibility. But Gordon eventually understood and grew to appreciate more and more what Chris was sacrificing for him. It was a pivotal point in our relationship.

"All my awards, all the schools I got into, I have Chris to thank for all of that," Gordon says. "During my senior year my friends were upset with me. I won practically every award Pine Crest had to offer. I won the Math & Science Award, the Harvard Book Award, the President's Award, and the Scholar Athlete of the Year Award. One of the awards I received for Broward County was the Brian Piccolo Award for scholar-athletes. In my acceptance speech, I said, 'If I reached any heights of achievement, it's because I've stood on the shoulders of a giant.' I was talking about Chris, the best brother I could ever ask for."

As Chris tells it, "I failed often, but Gordon never failed." Chris would fumble around, figure out how to succeed, and then give Gordon the game plan for what to do and how to do it. Gordon would then go full-out after it—he's never one to do anything halfway.

Years later, after Chris became CEO and was working with his business coach, they talked about those three years training for Gordon's wrestling seasons.

"You didn't know it at the time, Chris," his coach said, "but that was a multimillion-dollar investment you made. Your and Gordon's ability to work together at ChenMed was born out of that time together in the weight room and on a wrestling mat at Pine Crest."

THE SUMMER AFTER Gordon's senior year at Pine Crest and Chris's third year at UM (which was his first year of medical school), Chris decided that, in addition to the youth mission trip with the church, the two of us should go on a separate medical mission trip to Nicaragua.

"After my first year of medical school, I thought I was 'the smartest' I have ever been in my life," says Chris. "It was later, after my first year as an intern, that I realized I was 'the dumbest' I've ever been in my life."

With all the hubris of a first-year medical student, Chris talked with Gordon after his graduation. "Gordon, you're going to be a doctor," he said. "I'm almost one now. Let's go, you and me, to Nicaragua this summer. Instead of doing manual labor like we usually do on these trips, let's go make a difference. Let's go save lives."

We arrived in Nicaragua and met with Dr. Sirker, an American-trained physician who ran the medical mission and emergency services there. Chris explained our purpose in coming that summer.

"Good news, Dr. Sirker," Chris said. "I have some training now—I just finished my first year of medical school. Gordon and I are here to save lives."

"Show me the courses you've taken," he said.

He looked those over, looked us over, and nodded his head.

"Tomorrow morning, Chris and Gordon, I will pick you up at 6:00 a.m., and you can start the lifesaving work I have in mind for the two of you."

We got a good night's sleep and were up before dawn, ready to go. Dr. Sirker arrived with his pickup truck and directed us to hop in the back. He drove into the countryside. Nicaragua is extremely lush—like Hawaii. The land is rich with the volcanic ash. He pulled up to a beautiful clearing that stretched out at the base of one of Nicaragua's inactive volcanoes. Tropical birds filled the air with their good morning songs. We marveled at the thrill of God's artistic display, watching the sunrise paint the sky and landscape with a majestic palette of colors.

"Thank you, Dr. Sirker, for bringing us out to see the sunrise," said Chris. "It was stunning. What a great way to start our day!"

"Oh, I didn't bring you out here to see the sunrise," said Dr. Sirker. "See those two shovels and pickaxes in the back of the truck? We're going to build a huge, beautiful medical complex right here in this clearing. I need a water line, four feet deep and two feet wide, that runs from here"—he indicated where we were standing—"to there." He pointed off in the distance, about two hundred yards away. "I'll be back to pick you up just before dark."

Remember, we had both been working out every day—lifting weights and getting Gordon ready for football and wrestling. Dr. Sirker had taken one look at Chris's one year of medical school classes and another look at the biceps we both sported. It wasn't too hard a decision for him to figure out where he could best use our talents and training that summer.

For the next four days, we learned firsthand what makes Nicaragua so lush. Beneath the two inches of rich topsoil are four feet of volcanic rock. We would have been back in that clearing a fifth day, but during the night Chris spiked a high fever and began yelling like a crazy person with hallucinations. Gordon freaked out and called Dad, wondering what he should do.

"Get him home. Now!" Dad said.

It was dengue fever, a mosquito-borne illness. Dr. Sirker drove us to the airport, and we got the first flight home to Florida.

That was the only trip to Nicaragua we have ever taken as just the two of us. We've continued to go back each summer on some sort of mission trip with others ever since. Now on that twenty-acre property is an enormous medical complex, the home base for twenty-nine community clinics in Nicaragua.

"I realize that the trench Gordon and I dug that summer, providing water for the medical complex, has saved more lives, and will continue to save them for generations, than I ever could as a doctor, much less as a first-year medical student," said Chris. "I may have been clueless, but God knew what he needed from two strong, able-bodied Chinese boys that summer."

ONCE GORDON graduated from Pine Crest, Chris was able to focus his attention on medical school. In that next year, he went from the bottom to third in his class. Gordon, meanwhile, was making a tough decision. As we mentioned earlier, the expectation for most of our lives was that we would both follow Dad at UM's medical school's six-year program, then join him in his practice. Chris, without ever considering another option, had dutifully met the expectation. With his awards, academic achievements, and athletic accomplishments, Gordon had other options for college and medical school.

He was accepted into the UM six-year program. So far, so good. But he was also accepted at Yale, Harvard, and Brown University's prestigious eight-year medical degree program, the only Ivy League medical school you could enter as a freshman. Chris had not been accepted into that program. Would Gordon fall in line with the family's wishes and once again follow in Chris's trailblazing footsteps? Or would his first act of teenage rebellion and attempt to establish himself as his own man be to accept one of the other offers?

When Gordon was accepted at UM, Dad took the family out for dinner at one of Miami's nicest and most expensive restaurants, The Forge. Rather than a celebration, however, the whole night was spent fighting at the table. Gordon had made his decision.

"I'm doing my own thing, not following in your or my brother's footsteps anymore," he announced. "I'm going to Brown, and I'm going to play football."

Dad was extremely upset. He argued about the time it would take.

"Six years here in Miami, right here with your family. Eight years at Brown! It will take you longer to join the family practice!"

"I don't want the same path as you and Chris at UM. I can make my own path!" Gordon pronounced.

OUR PARENTS SHARED a strong faith-based belief system, and they sought to instill the values of that faith in us. In high school, Gordon was very involved at church, and he relied on

**101**

his faith to pull him through the academic, social, and athletic pressures he experienced in school. But in the very liberal environment of Brown, Gordon's faith was challenged. He drifted from his relationship with God in those first two years, so Dad found a church—arguably the most conservative church in Rhode Island—for Gordon to attend. On Sunday mornings he would show up to check that box, even though the six other days of the week he was partying and doing things inconsistent with a vibrant faith. So when Gordon's roommate and teammate, Drew Inzer, said he wanted to go to church with him one Sunday, Gordon was surprised but willing.

Drew had lots of questions for Gordon. Being so well trained in the Bible and faith from his earliest memories, Gordon knew how to answer all of Drew's questions. The problem for Gordon was that he wasn't living it himself. This challenged Gordon to look more closely at his own life. Drew publicly professed his faith, and he matured rapidly. Along with Gordon's girlfriend at the time, they started a Bible study group on the Brown campus—a highly unusual gathering in that student body.

Gordon realized it was time to step up—Drew had raised the bar even higher in terms of spiritual growth. Together, Gordon and Drew started a Bible study group among members of the football team, started training together, and encouraged one another to grow in spiritual maturity.

They also trained together and pushed one another as football players. From their sophomore year on, they both started on the varsity team. Brown won the Ivy League championship title their junior year. Going into their senior year, Gordon and Drew were co-captains. After a cold and grueling season, they finished their four years as the winningest team in Brown history. They were named to the All-Ivy and All-New England teams. Drew went on to play in the NFL and earned a Super Bowl ring with the New England Patriots in 2002.

As THEIR SENIOR season ended, Gordon was contemplating where he'd go for medical school. In addition to the option of staying at Brown, he had also applied to the University of Miami and Harvard Medical School, where he got an interview (an achievement in itself) but ultimately was not accepted. It was the first time in his life he hadn't gotten something he wanted.

Of course, Dad wanted him back in Miami, so when Providence, Rhode Island, entered the worst winter of Gordon's four years at Brown, Dad called up, asking, "How's the weather up there? You know, we're in shorts here in South Florida."

Gordon eventually decided to accept a scholarship and return to South Florida, following in the footsteps of Dad, Chris, and two uncles who had attended the University of Miami's medical school.

Once GORDON WAS back in Miami at medical school, Dad helped him and another first-year student organize another Nicaraguan medical mission trip. They prayed for days and days about it, and God faithfully opened all kinds of doors for them. The next year they did it again, and this time it was much easier to organize. A new first-year student, Jessica Lane, signed up. Gordon learned that Jessica was Jason Lane's sister, and she learned he was Chris's brother; it was a huge "aha" moment for them both. Gordon had been praying for his future wife since he was five or six. He knew almost immediately that he had found her. Highly intelligent, Jessica finished number one in her class in medical school. And yet, she did it without allowing medical school to consume her life. She worked out two hours a day. She attended church faithfully. She wasn't an alpha-female type, as so many women are forced to become if they want to survive in the highly competitive academic world of medical school, but she was humble and passionate about her faith in Christ. When she and Gordon started dating after that second Nicaraguan medical mission trip, both families were on board with them getting married.

CHRIS SAYS THAT he is the "dumb one" of the second generation of doctors in our family. He graduated all the way down at number three in his class. Gordon, who of course had to finish better than Chris, graduated second in his class. Jessica, not competing with anyone and simply being herself, was first in her class the following year.

GRADUATING THIRD in his class at UM's medical school didn't stop Chris from being admitted into Harvard Medical School's residency program. Focused on becoming a cardiologist, he had a life-changing experience while seeing a heart patient in the intensive care unit at Boston's Beth Israel Deaconess Medical Center.

He describes that whole period as a very challenging time for him.

During high school, he had started having questions about God. The more he learned intellectually as he went through college, medical school, and then residency, the more questions he had. They were metaphysical questions—where is the soul? Does the soul rely on something in the body? Is the soul created first and then the body, or is the body created and then a soul placed within it? How and why does something intangible, such as the human soul, rely on something tangible, such as the body?

Along with these metaphysical questions came questions about God. Where is God in all this? *What is God?* Chris began to struggle with bridging the gap between the worldly knowledge he was gaining and the faith that had been woven into the fabric of his childhood.

It all came to a head one night in the ICU at Beth Israel. Chris had gotten to know a lovely lady in her late sixties during his rotations. He had been reassuring her that she was getting better, that she looked good, and that she'd be leaving the ICU soon and would get to go home.

Then he got a call to go see her in the middle of the night. Anxious and scared, she wasn't feeling well. Again, exercising his best bedside manner, Chris told her not to worry. He had an EKG done and immediately thought, *Oh, my goodness! She's having a heart attack!*

Maintaining his outward composure, he told her what was happening, but that it was early and she was in the best place she could possibly be for this to happen. Chris got on the phone and called in the medical team—his professors and the attending cardiologist—who arrived within fifteen to twenty minutes. When someone is having a heart attack, medical professionals shift into a higher gear. Those parts of the heart that aren't getting blood flow are quickly dying.

Wheeling her into "the cath"—the catheterization lab or operating room—he explained that they would go in, find the blood clot that was causing the heart attack, and remove it from the artery.

"Your heart will experience minimal to no damage. You'll soon be well on your way to recovery," he said.

Chris was excited to be a part of saving her life. They got her on the table, prepared her for surgery, and made the incision. Then they inserted the catheter into her artery and fed it up into her heart. Knowing he wanted to be a cardiologist, and that he had made the proper diagnosis, the attending physician allowed Chris to participate, along with the cardiology fellow who was also in the room.

"Yep," the surgeon said. "There's the clot."

They saw it on the screen and used a device to suck it out. But just as that was happening, her heart stopped pumping.

Chris began to do chest compressions. With his size and strength, he was able to match her heart's normal beat, but if he stopped, so did her heart. He would pump her back to life, the cardiologist would tell him to stop to see if her heart responded, and she would die again.

She even woke up and tried to talk to Chris. She saw him pumping her heart and, naturally, was terrified. The team did everything they knew to do to get her heart to respond. Nine times Chris brought her back to life, and nine times her heart stopped—and she died.

"Finally, we knew we had to call it in," Chris says. "The last time she looked at me, all I could say was 'I'm sorry.'"

This same woman whom he had reassured many times that she was going to be OK was now gone. Nine times he had brought her back to life. Pressing, relevant questions about the soul haunted him. *When did her soul leave her body?* It was extremely difficult. His faith fell like a house of cards.

He and Stephanie had difficulty finding a church home in Boston. Desperate for relief and answers to his questions, Chris went on a skiing trip with Dad. Up late one night, he poured his heart out about the challenges he was facing with his faith.

"Son, you're overcomplicating things," Dad said.

Here's a man with a PhD who finished four years of medical training in two years, earned a master's degree in chemistry, was the number one student in Taiwan, and he's telling his son he's overcomplicating things. Chris remembers thinking at the time, *OK, this I've got to hear.*

"You have complicated questions," Dad said. "Let's go to the simple. Answer the simple first, then go from there. Every person must answer this question. Many don't because they're not intellectually consistent. But here's the question—*Did man create God or did God create man?* You must decide for yourself the answer to that question, and then be consistent with the implications of the answer you choose."

Chris was ready to hear where this was going.

"I can't prove to you that God created man, and I cannot prove to you that man created God," Dad continued. "But these are the only two possible options. This I can tell you. What we know about the universe, and how *finely tuned* the universe is, makes it very unlikely that man created God. The physics community is in a turmoil over this very thing. Those who want to deny God's existence twist themselves into knots trying to leave God out of the equation when they try to explain the origins of the universe. All that we really know now points to a creator. The honest physicists, through their work, are proving the presence of a creator God."

Dad let that sink in. He then presented the implications of the other answer.

"Now, what if man created God? If you go that route, again you must be intellectually consistent. Don't be like those hypocrites out there, who believe in one thing but behave differently."

With his penetrating, kind eyes, Dad looked at Chris.

"Here's what I mean," he said. "If man created God, there is no absolute truth. No transcendent truth above this world. There is no right and wrong; there are merely opinions. What you prefer may not be what I prefer. But neither of us can be outraged over questions of right and wrong. Maybe you don't prefer mass genocide. But what Hitler did cannot be called wrong if man created God. It is just one human being preferring something that others don't prefer. Remember, if man created God, then there can be no absolute truth. In fact, according to natural selection, if there is weakness, you should kill it! If you see someone with something you want, pick up a stone, bash them over the head, and take it! They're weaker—we shouldn't allow them to pass on their DNA. There's nothing wrong with that—just look at what happens in nature. It's the way the universe works. You may not prefer it if you're the person getting their head bashed in. But you can't say it's wrong. We're free to create any truth we want if there is no absolute truth. Absolute truth can only come from a God who created man."

Dad's argument was logical and rational. Chris knew he was hearing exactly what he needed to hear. Silence filled the room for a few minutes.

Then Dad delivered the implications of a world in which God created man.

"If God creates man, then you have a different problem," said Dad. "Now you have a Creator. And if you have a Creator, then that Creator must have a purpose for creating you, right? What's your purpose, Chris? And what's your relationship with your Creator? Shouldn't you ask your Creator to find out what your relationship should be and what your purpose is? Don't overcomplicate this. Keep it to the simple question. And then be consistent with your answer once you consider the implications of each possibility."

Chris remembers going back to his room to think it through. He reached his decision.

*I cannot live in a world, in fact I refuse to live in a world, where love, joy, transcendent truth, music, beauty, and art do not exist. The fact that I refuse to live in a world like that probably means that I was created!*

*Why would we long for these things to exist if they're not possible? We crave air because there is air! I'm hungry! Why? Because there's such a thing as food. Why do I crave love? Why do I want to give it? Why do I want to move closer to beautiful music when I hear it? Because it exists.*

*Why are we always in search of truth? Because it exists.*

As with just about everything else in life, Chris wrestled a bit harder than Gordon to come to a deep and abiding faith in the God who created the universe, who revealed Himself to us in the person of Jesus Christ, who continues to reveal Himself through the ongoing work of the Holy Spirit. But he decided that day: *There is a God. I was created. I need to figure out my relationship with my Creator and get to know Him.*

FOR BOTH OF US, God prepared us to have the faith in Him we would need when we got our calls about Dad's cancer. By then, we understood that we don't need to figure everything out in advance. Our job is to show up and let God do the work.

Today people come to see what we're doing at ChenMed. They think we're so amazing for coming up with this healthcare model.

We say, "No. That's not what happened. We've done what any logical person would do. And God has moved all the pieces. We didn't know that what we were doing would be the future of healthcare or if it would even work."

Now we ask, "What do You want to do with this, God?

Where do You want us to go? How do we make sure that we're not leading, but that You're leading?"

"I'm very much the kind of person who likes to lead!" says Chris. "But I have to work on getting out of the way so that God can lead. It's the same thing that happened in Wisconsin. Mom wanted to lead it. She and Dad learned the lesson—let God lead."

Every day we try to make sure we're following that lesson. And sometimes, the two of us have very strong differences of opinion as to which way God is leading. When the experts from McKinsey observed one of our battles over the company's direction, they described what we were doing as "violent agreement." A wise Jewish king, Solomon, once wrote, "Iron sharpens iron, and one man sharpens another" (Proverbs 27:17). We do the same thing that we did on the practice wrestling mats for three years at Pine Crest when we wrestle over tough decisions at ChenMed. We are two big, strong, Chinese jocks who learned to do our very best for ourselves, our family, our patients, and our God. And we will pour everything we have into making sure we're giving our best.

THERE'S ANOTHER PIECE of Jewish wisdom that has guided us through the years. Proverbs 21:31 says, "For the horse is prepared for the day of battle, but victory rests with the Lord."

We train, we exercise discipline, we prepare. And then we wait for God to move the infinite number of variables around in the ecosystem.

If we succeed, we say, "It's on You, God."

If we fail, it's not on us . . . *if* we've obeyed God's plan. Even our failures are for our good *if* we've sought for and obeyed His plan. Our faith is not blind—it's based on God's track record over our entire lives and all human history. Faith that cannot be tested cannot be trusted. We've learned that whatever we do, we are serving our God even as we serve our patients. We know we can do nothing less than bring our best. God is our Creator. Everything we do ultimately is for Him.

Chris's love of physics, informed by his faith and reading of the Bible, has led him to believe in a formula of the universe set in place by the one who created it all. When we are tested, when we go through trials, difficulties, and struggles, they can empower us and help us develop perseverance. When we persevere, we are shaped and formed into mature people of character. And as mature people of character, we are prepared to face anything life may throw at us with hope for the future.

As a family, Mom and Dad lived that formula through their experience of losing everything in Wisconsin and the years of struggle to get Dad through medical school and residency. The two of us proved the formula to be true from the streets of Liberty City to Harvard and Brown. Collectively, our family has proven it to be true from Dad's cancer diagnosis to where we are with ChenMed today.

Struggle that produces perseverance, perseverance that leads to mature character, mature character that offers hope— like gravity and Mom accomplishing anything she sets out to do—this formula is a truth of the universe.

# CHAPTER 5

# THE BEGINNING of TRANSFORMATIVE CARE

IT WAS BACK in 1984 that Dad finished his residency. Rather than joining someone else's staff or working at a hospital, he wanted his own private practice. Miami's North Shore Hospital had a program that sponsored new doctors with interest-free loans in North Miami Beach. If your practice was successful, you repaid the loan. If not, the loan was forgiven. The one thing they required was for doctors who received the loans to be on call at the hospital. This wasn't necessarily a bad thing—it gave Dad access to patients who didn't have a primary care physician (PCP) and the opportunity to bring them into his practice. He volunteered at another hospital for the same purpose—to build his patient base.

He wanted to establish his practice near North Shore but other PCPs complained, not wanting additional competition for patients. As a result, Dad was forced farther north. He began in the Sky Lake area, where he and Mom bought a house. Many of his early patients were elderly, transplanted New Yorkers, mainly Jewish people, who lived in the area's high-rise condos and apartments. Many of their children were doctors and lawyers in New York.

Because of his work at North Shore and the other hospitals close by, Dad also quickly became the PCP for many African Americans who visited the hospital emergency rooms without a doctor whom they saw on a regular basis. They were much poorer than the Jewish patients, but Dad's compassion and concern for them was apparent. They picked up on that, identified with him because of their shared minority status, and immediately told others about the new Chinese doctor who was providing excellent medical care for them and their loved ones.

For the first six months, Dad had no one working the front desk of his clinic. He had a couple of nurse assistants, but they were all busy in the back serving the influx of patients, frequently seeing up to thirty people a day. At the time, Dad was still operating his practice on the old model of fee for service—each time a patient came in, they paid for their appointment and services rendered. With no one sitting at the front desk, much of the cash the patients paid Mom and Dad was disappearing from the desk drawer and going out the front door before Dad could deposit it in the bank.

Mom was still working as a music teacher in the public school system. Dad approached her: "Mary, come work with me. I need you at my office."

"I don't know, Jim. I would be very uncomfortable having to answer the phone."

"Don't worry about that! All I ask is that you sit at the front desk and make sure our money doesn't disappear."

It didn't take long to see this was a very wise decision.

Dad says, "Within the first month, we saw that Mom sitting there recovered more money for us than she would have made as a music teacher in the public school."

It made economic sense. And with Mom's skill set and gifts, she quickly contributed much more than simply protecting the cash drawer. She took over, completely running the business side of Dad's practice. She knew who the "customers" were, and just as she had been so successful with her restaurants, she proved to be a warm, welcoming presence who got to know the patients and their families. Her genuine, generous spirit made them feel welcome and cared for. She and Dad were a great team.

At the end of the first year, Dad and Mom's hard work showed. They had completely paid off the loan from North Shore, and the practice was self-sustaining. Soon our parents realized that most of their patients coming in were African American, the population they felt called to serve—perhaps because they identified with them, but also because they recognized there was a great need. To serve these patients better, Dad decided to establish his practice in Miami Gardens, just west of I-95.

While it sounds lovely and bucolic, Miami Gardens is a poorer, more industrial part of North Miami. Some of his initial wealthier patients from Sky Lake didn't follow Dad across the interstate to Miami Gardens, preferring not to travel into that area. But Dad was fine with that—from the beginning of his practice, he felt called to help the underserved, and they embraced him and his care. Having lived in and been a part of that community in Liberty City while Dad was in training, we were comfortable with them and they with him. This is why we continue there today, and our corporate campus is right in the heart of Miami Gardens.

In THE EARLY 1990s, South Florida had become one of the centers of a new methodology for healthcare management—the health maintenance organization, or HMO. Humana was one of the first insurance companies to incorporate it, working with the United States government to offer Medicare Advantage. Because of Miami's older population, it didn't take long for half of the patients in the area to be on an HMO plan. Knowing that a large portion of Dad's practice was dedicated to seniors, Humana came to the office to ask if he would like to partner with them in this new way of providing healthcare.

Mom was at the front desk. She asked questions and found out that the company had two hundred patients to offer Dad's practice—patients who had been with other PCPs who no longer wanted to serve these patients. It turned out those PCPs were no longer making any money on them. Mom loved the idea of adding two hundred new patients to the books—but she recognized the financial risk they would take by accepting them.

Here's the catch for the PCP, which Dad would be, in this full-risk model. Rather than fee for service in which patients pay every time they see the doctor, the PCP is given a flat sum of money by Medicare Advantage for each patient based on the condition of their health. The PCP is then responsible for all of that patient's medical care. It's called full-risk for a reason—the PCP assumes all that risk. If your patient is healthy, stays out of the hospital, and doesn't have to see expensive specialists, it can be financially profitable for your medical practice. If, however, your patients are sickly and require hospitalization and specialized care, any additional costs come out of your pocket as the PCP. Mom and Dad had to make a business decision for the practice. And with primarily seniors for patients, this would be a very risky venture.

Most PCPs who accepted the HMO challenge tried to make their money by seeing patients as little as possible. Mom talked it over with Dad. If these other doctors couldn't make a profit with these patients, how would they?

Dad met with two cardiologists in the area, the Fox brothers, who had over a thousand patients on an HMO plan. They had worked out a system that allowed them to make their practice profitable. One of the important lessons he learned from them was that when he did expand his practice to hire more doctors, the quality of those doctors was most important.

"Hire the best doctor, not a lousy one!" they said.

After meeting with the Fox brothers several times, Dad felt confident that he could make the HMO model work.

He said to Mom, "I know what to do. What these other

doctors are doing is trying *not* to see their patients in order to make money. We will do the opposite. We will make sure our patients come to see us more often. We will practice prevention rather than merely treating symptoms and disease. All we need to do is cut down the waste. We will provide the care that others are sending to a specialist. We'll get them healthy so they don't need to see a specialist."

The first month with these new patients, Mom and Dad had a surplus from the HMO. Dad called both of us—we were still completing our educations.

"Don't you worry. I have money to pay for school!"

DAD DIDN'T HAVE to change his philosophical approach to providing healthcare under this new model. It was entirely consistent with how he treated his patients. He and Mom did worry in those first months if they had made the right decision. But at the end of every month, somehow it all worked out. They prayed and kept their faith. They continued to improve their systems, to cut waste and improve patient care.

"Just as before, I treated all patients the same," Dad says. "Whatever they needed, we offered. In the prior fee-for-service model, you can't see your patients very often because they can't afford it. With this new full-risk model, I could see my patients as often as necessary. Humana gave me no restrictions on how often I saw my patients. They gave me a flat fee, and it was up to me and the patient as to how often I saw them to keep them healthy."

With his new, frequent care model, Dad soon saw

evidence of reduced hospital visits for his patients. It was better for the patients, and it was better for the practice.

"You take care of patients like you take care of your grandfather," Dad says. "And if you do the right thing, you will make money doing it."

He worked very hard at it. Dad sometimes needed to be at the hospital with a patient at 11:00 p.m. He would call Mom, who had been at the office all day and was the last person to leave and lock up, with a request.

"Mary, please drive the boys to the ER so I can spend some time with them."

When Dad is asked how he was able to work such long hours with a young family, he always gives the same answer.

"I have a very supportive wife!"

In those days before cell phones, busy professionals used pagers—a device that you could wear on your belt, with its own phone number, which would beep when someone called you to let you know they had left you a message. He gave his pager number to his patients so that they could call him at any time. He was fully committed to improving their health through diet, a carefully monitored medical regimen, and prayer. Despite what other doctors expected, Dad and Mom thrived from a business standpoint.

He developed a culture of excellence and accountability, and he started with himself. If a patient was sick, he wanted to see them every day. No matter what issue they may have, he said, "Come in to see me tomorrow."

"Frequency of seeing the patient is a matter of need," he

explains. "I soon learned that once a month is a minimum. With seniors, many of whom are on five to ten medications, I needed to see them more often to make sure the medications were working and not causing a bigger problem because of negative interactions."

Just talking to patients on the phone wasn't enough. There's no substitute for eyeballing a patient to see how they're doing. Often older patients don't realize they're not doing well. By seeing them frequently in person, Dad could tell if their ankles were swelling, for example, or if they were experiencing other side effects.

"They wouldn't know there was a problem until they collapsed," he says. "But by having someone on staff check their blood pressure, ask the right questions, and look them over, we could stop small problems before they got bigger."

Other doctors in the area continued to see that Dad was willing to care for patients they no longer wanted on their books.

"Go see that Chinese doctor in Miami Gardens," they would say. "He loves to take care of really sick patients!"

They thought Dad was naïve at best—they didn't understand how his business of preventative medical care actually worked.

BECAUSE DAD intended for both of us to go to medical school and join him in the practice, early on he would take us with him on hospital visitations. From time to time, he would also take us on a home visit. We saw firsthand the impact he had on his patients in their homes—their anxiety immediately dissipated with his presence.

Gordon remembers carrying Dad's doctor bag for him on one home visit.

"I literally saw the change in the patient's face," Gordon says. "There was relief and hope, which they experienced with Dad's care. When Dad touched them, a calm and peace came over that person. I believe that touch and sincere care themselves lead to healing in patients. Knowing someone cares, someone who understands their condition and how to address it, is a powerful source for producing wellness in patients."

Mom ran all the nonmedical, business aspects of the practice. She was office manager, finance person, personnel director, head of sales—she did everything except medically treat patients. She took a no-nonsense approach to taking care of patients. Remember, from her Chinese culture, she and Dad had a profound respect for elders. They were brought up to love, heal, honor, and support them. She had high standards for herself, and she demanded a lot from the people who worked for her. For everyone, the focus was on taking the best possible care of the patients.

Mom was on top of everything. When patients came in each month, she would talk with them, asking how they were doing and how their families were doing. When we asked her how she did it, balancing numerous responsibilities all those years, she says, "Diddi and I depended on God to give us the strength we needed. It was only by God's grace and mercy! We were young, and we did have a lot of energy. We were just doing what we needed to do."

Who is "Diddi"?

Growing up, we both thought that this was the Chinese word for *Daddy*. One Sunday at the Chinese Baptist Church, one of us spoke about Dad and called him "Diddi."

"Why do you call him that?" a Chinese kid asked.

"Well, that's Chinese for *Daddy*," we said.

"No, it isn't!" the kid said.

"Yes, it is!" we insisted.

After arguing back and forth for a while, like kids do, the two of us began to question whether we were right or not. We went to Mom.

"Mommi, how do you say 'Daddy' in Chinese?" we asked.

"Bàba."

"Bàba?" we said, starting to get the picture. "Then how do you say 'Daddy' in English?"

"Diddi!" she exclaimed confidently, without skipping a beat. "Diddi" remains Dad's endearing nickname for our wives and kids to this day.

AMONG HER MANY responsibilities, Mom did all the financial analyses for the practice. Because of the high-risk element of the business model, she had to stay on top of monthly financial reports. At the end of every month, Humana sent a thousand-page printout itemizing every charge going against their Medicare Advantage accounts.

She discovered that specialists would charge them for a service they hadn't provided. Going over every report, page by page, one item at a time, she found that up to 50 percent of what they were being charged were mistakes. When we asked Dad how they handled that, he didn't have to think about the answer.

"Mom was never intimidated by insurance companies. She would go to their office and yell at them. She would make them get it right. In fact, she was so good at finding errors, she taught them how to better use their system."

Mom says, "I told them, 'If you make fewer mistakes, I have more time to do my work at my office, and you don't have to deal with me every month. You do it the right way, and we will all be better off.'"

At the end of the first year, she, Humana, and Aetna, which had also begun sending Dad HMO patients, had cut down the billing mistakes by 50 percent. She helped them improve their financial reports, fixing errors that were being made by incorrectly entering codes into the system. Those two insurance companies saved millions of dollars with Mom's assistance.

As the face of the practice at the front desk, Mom also dealt with and took good care of health plan agents and brokers. She made them feel comfortable—if they sent patients to ChenMed, those patients would be well taken care of. This was a crucial part of acquiring new patients and developing a reputation once they came into the practice. She and Dad made the agents look good because the patients would go back to tell them how happy they were with the referral.

LIKE IN EVERY real estate decision, *location, location, location* has played an important role in ChenMed's success. Miami's geography is a bit unique. As the city grew during the 1950s and '60s, the growth had to happen either to the north or the south of the city. The Atlantic Ocean prevents growth to the east, and farms and the Everglades are a barrier to the west. (Sadly, that barrier was pushed much farther west in the 1980s and '90s when developers began building gated communities.)

As we've mentioned before, when I-95 was built, it became the divider of neighborhoods and socioeconomic communities. Toward the beach you found the affluent residents living on higher priced, more valuable real estate. The poorer neighborhoods were pushed west.

Golden Glades is a neighborhood where three major highways come together—I-95, the Florida Turnpike, and the Palmetto Expressway. Miami Gardens was caught in that division, just west of I-95. In the fifties and sixties, it had been a middle-class neighborhood. With the building of those highways, the middle-class people left. When Dad was pushed north from North Shore and started his practice in that area, Golden Glades had become very industrial and commercial.

About the same time that he and Mom switched the practice to an HMO model, they rented the entire fifth floor of a building there. It was a multi-use building, with a variety of businesses in it. But over several years Dad built out his floor, adding his own beautiful lab, exam rooms, and a nice waiting and front desk area.

From Dad's initial staff of a couple of nurse assistants, between 1993 and 2003 the practice grew to twenty-five employees including nurse practitioners, lab technicians, and four doctors. The first doctor they ever hired walked in off the street and asked

Mom if they had an opening for another doctor. He said he was working in another practice, but he was having to do administrative work. He said, "Just give me a salary and let me see patients."

Knowing how hard Dad was working with all the patients, she told him about the visitor. Dr. Channer was hired and worked for ChenMed for more than twenty years, right up until he retired.

After ten years in that space on the fifth floor, with a very successful clinic clicking along under Dad and Mom's excellent supervision, the building was sold to a group wanting to convert the whole facility into an Orthodox Jewish school. Mom and Dad had negotiated a long-term lease, but the new owners wanted ChenMed out, and they were willing to go to rather extreme measures to achieve their desired end.

The first thing they did was shut off the air conditioning during South Florida's notoriously hot summer. Trust us—you don't want to be on the fifth floor of an enclosed building in Miami with no air conditioning at any time, much less the summer. When that didn't convince Mom and Dad to move the practice, they shut down the elevators, forcing elderly patients to walk up five flights of stairs.

Of course, Dad and Mom were extremely upset. They couldn't allow this for their patients or their staff. When they complained repeatedly, the new owners invited them to take their case to court. Not willing to sue and drag it out for who knows how long, they decided to look for a new facility.

Just before moving to the new location, we found out about Dad's cancer. It was during the time that Chris was coming down on weekends from New York that he was able to help Mom move the practice into a new building, also in Miami Gardens. With Dad in Houston for treatments, a friend who specialized in IT helped set up the computers.

At that time, there were about twelve hundred patients in the practice. Just as ChenMed benefited from the castoffs—patients whom other doctors didn't want to serve—the same happened with the doctors Dad and Mom were able to hire. Some other practices didn't want foreign doctors in their practice.

Mom and Dad said, "We'll take them."

Remembering the Fox brothers' advice, Dad's only criteria was that they were great doctors with a passion to provide the very best preventative care they could for their patients. If they were willing and able to maintain Dad's standards of excellence, he couldn't care less about their country of origin. Drs. Alfonso and Bui joined Dad and Dr. Channer and are still with us. The team was intentional in offering VIP care to every patient who walked through the doors.

OF COURSE, even with this excellent staff, Dad was the star doctor seeing patients. Once he became sick, the clinic was like a professional sports team that loses its star player to an injury. During his cancer treatments, rather than just sitting on the sidelines, Dad went into full-time coaching and development. He focused on strategy and technology. Under Dad's tutelage, performance didn't diminish. It improved.

Dad went from working *in* the business to working *on* the business.

No longer preoccupied by seeing one patient at a time, he was able to focus on developing technology and systems that allowed more patients to be seen more effectively. The PhD scientist applied his understanding and grasp of how to use data to develop an even better system for patient care. Dad pored over printouts of each doctor's patient panel (the number of patients a doctor sees as their PCP) and came up with an ideal range of 400 to 450. He saw that our doctors could comfortably see 20 patients a day. With an average of twenty-two working days in a month, that gives a total of 440.

The design was for every doctor to see every patient every month. This was groundbreaking—nonexistent in the medical world before Dad's model. Now if a patient goes into the hospital, the first question their PCP is asked is, "Were you seeing your patient every month?"

There's positive peer pressure among our doctors to stick to it. Just as Dad did when he started his practice, our doctors hold one another accountable to a minimum of monthly in-person exams for every patient. The data he studied on all the doctors proved it—if you push patient visits out too long, they get sick.

Some doctors can only see three hundred patients a month— and if that's what they can do comfortably and still maintain their patients' good health, so be it. We've tried going as high as five hundred, but outcomes suffered, so now the top limit for patient panels has been set at that 450 level.

Dad also learned that, across all his doctors and their patients, this improved the patient-doctor relationship. When they're seen every month by their PCP, patients feel cared for. If they are sick, it gives them hope that they'll get better. This is an important part of getting and staying well. Also, when our patients have more opportunities to see their doctor, they're more likely to follow through on what the doctor asks them to do. They realize it won't be long until they're asked if they've been following their protocol. There's accountability for both the doctor and the patient— the doctor to see how the patient is doing and the patient to follow through on what the doc has recommended to achieve and maintain good health.

During his sickness, when Dad was studying the data he'd accumulated, he realized he needed a better system to track how doctors were doing with their patients. Not only did he want to know how many patients each doctor was seeing per day, but, how long patients were having to wait to be seen. Where was the bottleneck? And how could it be opened up?

Dad developed a tool to take all the data he had for each doctor and all that came in from the insurance companies, and he instituted a business intelligence department. He integrated multiple software programs for every aspect of ChenMed's services. There was a section for all hospitalized patients, one for referrals, one for specialists, and one for home care, with a separate program designed for each area. In all, he wrote two hundred programs that all work together and give us the information we need to better care for our patients.

THE FIRST YEAR after Dad's cancer diagnosis, Chris came home often during Dad's treatments. After the treatments ended, he

Mom and Dad on their wedding day in 1971.

Mom and Dad in Wisconsin in 1977.

Mom and her boys after arriving in Miami.

Here are the two of us on the wrestling mats
at Pine Crest School. Can you tell who is who?

Chris is helping Gordon stretch before
the 1997 State Wrestling Championship.

We were able to play together for one year on the Pine Crest School varsity football team. Mom and Dad were our biggest cheerleaders.

Chris married Stephanie in 1999. Gordon, the best man,
and Stephanie's sister, the maid of honor,
are the photobombers in the background!

Chris's University of Miami Medical School graduation.

The family is all together at one of Gordon's
Brown University football games.

Dad, Chris, and Gordon are at Gordon's
University of Miami medical school graduation.

Here are all of us on Gordon and Jessica's wedding day in 2003.
We just found out Dad's cancer was treatable.

The *Miami Herald* featured Mom and Dad
in the early days of ChenMed.

Chris, Stephanie, and the kids in Miami.
What do you think of these shades?

Gordon, Jessica, and the kids in 2018.
Someone didn't get the memo to dress in solid blue.

Chris and Stephanie in Colorado in 2019.

Gordon and Jessica in 2020.

Mom and Dad's 50th wedding anniversary in 2021.

Chris, Stephanie, Jessica, and Gordon posed for
the 2021 ChenMed holiday card.

The three most important women in our lives:
Stephanie, Jessica, and Mom.

didn't have to come as often and was able to finish his three-year fellowship with no delay. Jessica and Gordon, in school at UM, were able to spend every weekend with Mom and Dad, helping any way they could.

This was a very critical time for ChenMed. No longer was it just Mom and Dad running that first center—the whole family was now not only working on the business, but also working together on something much bigger.

It was always a dream of Dad's to have more sites to be able to see more patients. His sickness accelerated that transition. As Chris was finishing his fellowship, he was excited to be coming home to fulfill the dream Dad had shared with him when he was five years old. Chris had gone through the six-year medical school program at UM. Now he would be working as a doctor with Dad. But in talking with Dad about how things would work when he was back in South Florida, Dad threw a wrench in Chris's understanding of the plan.

"Every lion needs his own cage," Dad said.

"What?" Chris started to argue. "I thought we would work together at the center."

"Every lion needs his own cage," Dad repeated. "We will be working together. But it's time to expand and open a second center. You need your own space."

"Well, will you help me build my cage?" Chris asked.

"Mom and I are Chinese. We are frugal," Dad said. "We have saved money, so yes—we will help you build your cage. Not only that—you can have Mom to go with you to help."

"Done!" Chris said.

With our parents' financial backing, Mom's administrative brilliance, and a couple of the doctors from the first clinic, ChenMed Center number two was primed for success and ready to be launched. It was brilliant forethought on Dad's part and the opposite of how most fathers who start a business handle a transition to their son.

Because Gordon and Jessica were local, with Gordon in his internship and Jessica finishing med school, they were able to allocate some time to locate property for the second clinic while Chris finished his fellowship in New York. We didn't want it to be too far from the original site—the plan was to move 30 to 50 percent of the existing patients to the new location, and then grow the patient base in both facilities. The site needed to be close to where many of our patients lived and where there was a large population of seniors who could get to the facility with ease.

We found a property we thought was perfect, about four miles from the Miami Gardens center. When we took it to Humana, however, that plan was nixed. They said it was too close to one of their other practices so we couldn't have it. This felt like a huge setback at first. Once again, ChenMed was going to get the leftovers and not our first choice. Dad and Gordon looked for an alternative site, finally secured another location in the Miami Lakes area, and began the process of setting up ChenMed Center number two.

It "just so happened" that Jessica was in her fourth year of med school at the time, which, while not easy by any means, did offer flexibility with her schedule and courses. She was allowed to take a one-month elective in business, which she was able to use helping open site number two. She developed an Excel spreadsheet listing every bit of inventory needed to open another center. That proved very helpful for future expansion as well.

Gordon, now an intern, also had time that he could devote to getting the new location ready for patients. He and Jessica assembled chairs, bought and installed the numbers for the exam room doors (Jessica says, "Those numbers are still a little crooked!"), and put sticky letters on a big mirror that describes a truth that continues to inform ChenMed's approach to medical care today:

*A patient IS not an interruption of our work—they are the purpose of it. We are not doing our patients a favor by serving them. They are doing us a favor by giving us the opportunity to do so.*

THIS QUOTATION isn't original to us. We "borrowed" it from a sign at MD Anderson in Houston, and no one can say with confidence where it originated. A mirror with that lettering became a signature of ChenMed centers. We moved two of the doctors from the original Miami Gardens location, along with half of our patients, and opened our second center.

The change of location caused by Humana *not* letting us have our first choice proved to be a blessing rather than a setback. The first site ran into a zoning issue, and its building was delayed by more than a year. Our new site quickly flour-ished—God had once again taken great care of us.

THE SECOND CENTER opened in 2006. By that time, Chris had just finished his fellowship and moved back to South Florida to dedicate all his talent and energy to ChenMed's success. After seeing how well number two had done, Chris went to Mom and Dad to ask if he could do it again with a third center. They said "Sure." We decided location three should be about the same distance from Miami Gardens as number two, with the original center in the middle and number three a few miles in the opposite direction in North Miami Beach. Gordon and Jessica again helped find the loca-tion, but because of their medical training commitments—with Gordon now in his cardiology fellowship and Jessica in residency—it made it difficult for them to have the time to offer much help otherwise.

Unlike site number two, where we sent two doctors from the original center, number three was the first completely organic startup—all-new staff and doctors to run it. We had a great location with a beautiful building, but the results were opposite of site number two. Whenever anyone walked through the doors, for over a year all you would hear were crickets. There were practically no patients.

Two million dollars of our parents' money had been invested in a state-of-the-art medical facility, but Chris and another doctor had almost nothing to do. Mom and Dad were very concerned, of course. The cost of maintaining such a large facility, fully staffed, was unsustainable if we didn't have any patients to serve.

Later, Mom joked about it. "Chris, I helped you with the second center. But do you know why I didn't come to the third? It was too depressing!"

It was a critical point in our business. ChenMed could have ended right there. Chris met with Dad to talk it over and come up with a plan.

"Why don't you go out into the community," Dad said, "and see if there are any doctors who are willing to join us and bring their patients with them?"

With Mom and Dad's money on the line, Chris started showing up in primary care physicians' offices within a five-mile radius, without an appointment, asking to see the lead doctor in the practice.

"Hello, I'm Dr. Chen. May I speak with Dr. So-and-so?"

Chris learned quickly to accept rejection. At one of the offices, the doctor's wife was the office manager, similar to Mom's role with Dad. She came out and started yelling at Chris, lecturing him.

"Who do you think you are? Coming in here, trying to take my husband's practice!"

Her diatribe went on for almost an hour. Chris stood there, took his medicine, and eventually went on to the next clinic. It was run by Dr. Larry Katz, who met Chris at the door.

"Dr. Katz, my name is Dr. Christopher Chen. I work with my dad, Dr. James Chen. We have three clinics to serve primarily the senior populations in North Miami. It's a beautiful and very different model for providing care to these patients." He went on to describe Dad's vision and methods, the awesome success we were experiencing in centers one and two, and the opportunity to do the same in center three.

"Would you be interested in being a part of something so beautiful?" Chris asked Dr. Katz. This precious Jewish doctor, balding, about five foot, three inches tall, looked up toward heaven, raised his hands, and said, "Thank you, God!"

He went on to explain to Chris that the corporation running his clinic was on the verge of shutting down his practice. The two of them talked, and Dr. Katz came on board at center three, bringing five hundred patients with him. The service these patients received at our North Miami Beach center was unlike anything they had experienced before. They started telling their friends, and word-of-mouth advertising by the patients themselves required us to hire another doctor to maintain our doctor-to-patients ratio.

That initial setback at the beginning of center three proved to be what catapulted us into much greater success. Dad and Chris taught Dr. Katz our methods. Mom came along to help absorb five hundred patients at one time and give them concierge, Ritz-Carlton–level service. Center three flourished, and the model for ChenMed expansion began to reveal itself.

WITH CHRIS applying his business knowledge and savvy to Dad's brilliant systems for providing the most excellent medical care possible, he continued to grow the practice by adding new patients and new sites. Chris and Mom pushed the

VIP service approach to generate patient referrals, and they had tight engagement with community sales agents who brought new patients. We were on a roll and Chris led the discovery of two new locations, both two-story buildings—center four in Hallandale, which opened in South Florida in 2008, and center five in North Miami, which opened in 2009. In six years, we grew from twelve hundred patients in one location to eight thousand patients in five locations. And it was accomplished with no drop in the quality of care we offered our patients or their satisfaction with the services we provided. We spent time educating doctors, getting them to see Dad's beautiful vision and his scalable model that deeply impacts seniors' lives. Some doctors didn't work out—especially those who had difficulty pivoting from fee-for-service to value-based care. But overall, we were able to recruit doctors successfully and maintain Dad's high standards of excellence in medical care.

Getting the right fit with our doctors has been critical to our success. Mom and Dad did the heavy lifting with those first hires and by establishing the highest of standards. Remember Mom's advice to Chris and Stephanie for raising children?

"It is not possible for you to set high enough expectations."

That same philosophy has been applied to our staff for the care of our patients. Doctors must be mission driven. They must care about seniors, who continue to be our primary patients. They must be teachable—willing to learn our formula and approach to patient care. And they should be upset about America's existing healthcare system, which burns out doctors and offers no long-term benefit for patients.

We look for doctors who want smaller patient panels (the number of patients one doctor can effectively manage). By setting a maximum number of patients for each doctor, we can go deeper with the patients we have. And with that smaller number, our doctors build trusting, beautiful relationships with each patient. This produces a positive, lasting impact on patient outcomes.

We also look for doctors who are humble, mission driven, and want to grow and lead. Gordon and Jessica identified many great physicians with these qualities during their training days at University of Miami (UM) Miller School of Medicine and Jackson Memorial Hospital.

Gordon noticed Dr. Maina Gatonye as a good fit for our vision and mission. He introduced Dr. Gatonye to Chris, Mom, and Dad. Dr. Gatonye joined us and today remains one of ChenMed's leading lights of medical care for patients. Other top physicians from Jessica and Gordon's medical school and residency training who continue to have key roles in ChenMed include Drs. Reyan and Alina Ghany, Dr. Roberto Ochoa, Dr. Gianni Neil, Dr. Rene Parraga, and Dr. Hermena Cerphy. All have key roles leading our clinical operations and clinical support teams.

Furthermore, other stars from their relationship with UM/ Jackson Memorial continue to embrace ChenMed's vision and mission. These more recent recruits include former chief residents Drs. Alexandria Beranger and Elizabeth Vilches-Olivera. Along with Drs. Carlos Trejos, Susan Schayes, Jorge Alfonso, and Len Scarpinato, they make an all-star team that has helped create a strong clinical culture that has helped us recruit other top talent. All are now actively engaged in attracting and developing other top physicians through relationships with additional top clinical programs like Emory University/Grady Hospital. Former department chiefs Drs. Susan Schayes and Nathan Flacker continue to help prospective physicians make the move to value-based care.

WHEN WE OPENED center number five, Jessica had just finished her residency and was able to come on board as an MD at that location. She loved serving as a PCP, which she did with half her time, and spent the other half of her time in administration for that center. Gordon was completing his fellowship in cardiology at the time. Along with his work for the five centers in South Florida, Chris started a new business consulting service—PMR, or Practice Management Resources, helping other medical practices set up and run a successful business model.

With that new business doing extremely well, we opened a sixth and then a seventh center in South Florida. Furthermore, due to our local success and high-quality outcomes, one of our health plan partners engaged us in an opportunity to expand beyond South Florida. By early 2011, JenCare Senior Medical Centers in Virginia was born.

# CHAPTER 6

# GO WEST (and NORTH), YOUNG MEN

THROUGHOUT THIS JOURNEY, from our father's battle with cancer to our medical practice's rapid growth, there have always been folks who give us too much credit for what we have accomplished. But we know the truth. Each day we put our trust in God and watch doors open and close that would never have moved with our own abilities. Something greater is happening. We're humbled that God has chosen to use us in a way that helps provide love and health to so many in tremendous need.

It is true that in a period of fifteen years we went from one clinic in South Florida to more than eighty in twelve states. It's also true that we are trying to lead the charge in transforming how healthcare is delivered and administered, while transforming care of the neediest populations—and that includes trying to eliminate racial disparities through healthcare. But did we know when we started that social injustice would be the number one issue in the hearts and on the minds of so many in America today? Of course not!

We wish we could tell you that we planned all this from the very beginning, but it would be a lie. We wake up every morning and simply do what God puts in front of us to do, using all the resources He gives us to do it. And He has blessed our efforts many times over, moving the entire ecosystem around us to enable and empower us to accomplish amazing things.

AROUND THE SAME time that Chris was leading the charge in growing our base in South Florida to five clinics, Christopher Ciano was named the new CEO of Coventry, one of the insurance companies we were working with. The two Chrises hit it off right away. Just as God had brought McKinsey consultants Bob Kocher and Todd Johnson into Chris's life, Ciano came along at just the right time, when everything was in place for us to make our next move.

Ciano was very impressed with our South Florida clinics. Chris would ask him questions about the business side of healthcare, and Ciano taught him more of the principles and business concepts necessary to run a successful practice. When Chris asked him if our model of providing healthcare could help other practices, doctors who were struggling with their business model, Ciano said, "Absolutely!"

Out of that initial conversation, Chris came to Mom

and Dad and asked for two million dollars to launch Primary Medical Resources, or PMR, a consulting company to advise primary care physicians on how to run a profitable, effective clinic. Mom and Dad, always so generous and willing to take a risk and trust Chris to follow through with his ideas, agreed. Ciano played a significant role getting the new business started by recommending PMR to several practices with whom he did business. Chris hired two extremely smart and savvy McKinsey consultants to come on board and do much of the work.

PMR was almost immediately successful. It didn't take long until we were working with 20 percent of Coventry's practices as well as a number of Humana's. It was through this work that the "franchise" business model for providing primary healthcare came into focus. ChenMed's clinics were thriving. Things were going great for us as a business, with our patient- and wellness-focused approach to providing healthcare reaching many more people through PMR than we could in our own centers.

THERE WAS ONE difficult relationship, however, that we were dealing with, and the source of it was one person. The person running Humana's South Florida operations at that time was treating ChenMed like a fourth-class citizen. He would humiliate Mom, talk down to her, and give preferential treatment to larger primary care groups. Whenever we wanted to open a new center, he did everything he could to make it difficult. His agenda was obvious—limit our growth and strengthen the primary care groups in his inner circle.

Chris went to Humana's offices to meet with Terry Smith, Humana's South Florida Chief Medical Officer, and several other key officers (including the CFO) to discuss what we were doing with PMR in some of their other practices. Unbeknownst to the person running Humana South Florida, the company's national corporate officers were frustrated and concerned about reports of compliance and fraud issues emanating from his office. On that very day, they had folks down from their headquarters in Louisville to replace "Mr. Difficult" and assess how to fix their Florida mess.

Not long after Chris's meeting began, a man came in, sat down, put his hands behind his head, and just listened to what was being said. He didn't introduce himself and no one introduced him—but Chris immediately picked up on the fact that this was someone important. The Florida officers sat up a little taller in their seats when he entered the room and seemed intimidated by his presence. Chris learned later that Bruce Perkins, one of the top three guys from Humana corporate, had come into this meeting to see if this was one more thing he was going to have to clean up.

He listened as Chris explained what was going on with ChenMed, PMR, and our relationship with Humana. Finally, the man spoke up and introduced himself.

"Chris, my name is Bruce Perkins. I'm here from the Louisville office. By any chance . . . are your parents Jim and Mary Chen?"

"Yes," Chris replied.

Perkins's face lit up.

"Hot dog!" he said. "I contracted with them fifteen to twenty years ago in my early years with Humana. I know exactly who they are."

Perkins was confident that Mom and Dad were not part of "Mr. Difficult's" inner circle of trouble. In other words, they weren't part of the problem. At the same time, a light bulb turned on for him, sensing that we could be a part of the solution.

"Chris," he went on, "what I've seen here, what you've shared, is really cool. Can I come visit you?"

We were nervous at first. But when Perkins came to see us, Chris walked him through one of our centers and showed him everything. Perkins was extremely impressed with our many innovations—advanced technology, using robots to deliver medications, all the centers being run efficiently and cost effectively, and with excellent health results for our patients.

"I see that you're not a typical South Florida practice," Perkins said at the end of their time together. "That's why you're growing so fast, and it's why you're producing the top results in all of Florida. I have an idea I would like to run by you."

PERKINS AND HUMANA corporate had just tried to buy a company in Southern California called CareMore, which had developed a scalable model for growing healthcare clinics that Humana wanted to expand nationally. Just as they were about to close the deal, however, another company swooped in and paid a 10 to 20 percent premium for a total of $790 million, taking the business away from Humana. Perkins saw in us and our model the potential to grow even more than CareMore. He believed that we had put in place the infrastructure necessary to replicate our South Florida successes.

On our part, that had been intentional. Chris had previously met with Karl Kellner, McKinsey's healthcare expert, in New York City. Chris told him about his dream for creating a healthcare model that could replicate nationally, but Kellner tried to burst his bubble. "I have two pieces of bad news, Chris," he said. "First of all, there's no such thing as a nationally scalable healthcare delivery model. It's always local. Why hasn't someone else thought of this and done it? Because it just won't work."

Chris listened attentively, but he wasn't convinced. Kellner continued.

"The second reason it won't work is because your full-risk value business only works in three markets in the US—Southern California, a few places in South Texas, and where you are in South Florida. Everyone—and I mean, *everyone*—who has tried to move out of these areas has failed miserably. Just don't do it. If you do, it will fail."

Chris took this feedback to his favorite place to process information—the ski slopes!

Bob Kocher, Todd Johnson, and Chris are all passionate, black diamond skiers. They would go on weekend skiing expeditions, and on the chairlift heading up to the top of the mountain, they would process how businesses other than healthcare providers were able to replicate. If they could do it, why couldn't we? Chris says those chairlift rides were some of the most productive business meetings he ever sat in on. The three of them came up with a strategy and model for a scalable system of delivering Dad's method of providing high-quality, life-changing healthcare.

"Take a pause, Chris," Kocher said. "Really assess where you are and if it will be possible to scale up. Nail it down and do it right! I believe that what your family is doing really can work. But get everything perfectly in place before you grow anymore. Before things get too complex, you want to make a good decision about going any further."

That's when Bruce Perkins reentered the scene. "I want to bring down several of our other key decision-makers from Louisville," Perkins told Chris. "We need to make this happen."

That next visit was the scariest day of our business lives. Along with Perkins was Jim Murray, the COO, and several others; they arrived on their private jet. Like Perkins, the others were impressed with our centers and our model for growth and scalability, and we signed a deal to partner with Humana and expand into five more states.

WITH HUMANA'S HELP, we identified Richmond and the Tidewater area as the places in Virginia with the most under-served and neediest senior populations. In a very bold move, and with Humana's investment as well as our own from the profits we garnered from PMR, we decided to start with five centers—two in Richmond and one each in Norfolk, Newport News, and Portsmouth.

As we made plans to launch this new partnership, we ran

focus groups to consider what we should call the new centers. Because of the heavy presence of retired military in this area, many of those we hoped to serve had fought in wars against Asians. We knew it was nothing personal against us, but our Chen last name had negative connotations in Tidewater. Not wanting the name to be a barrier preventing anyone from getting great healthcare, we settled on JenCare Senior Medical Centers. This was to honor Dad, whose Chinese name is Jen-ling, and it sounds much more American than Chen.

This all happened when Gordon was finishing his cardiology fellowship. He took on the role of recruiting doctors and identifying the sites for these five new centers. Not only was it something we had never done, it was something no one else had ever done! How do you get doctors to come work in a new clinic, with no building yet, in a state we've never worked in? It required a lot of vision-casting. We flew potential doctors down to Florida to see how our existing centers were run. For a brief time, the two of us and our wives moved to Virginia to get the lay of the land and help launch the new centers.

Very early on, we realized that this would be vastly different from our South Florida experience. The sites were much more spread out geographically as well as culturally, making this a more diverse and difficult market to serve. We learned that seniors don't like to cross tunnels and bridges to get to their healthcare provider—and there are lots of tunnels and bridges in the Tidewater area. Patients were poorer and needed transportation to get to and from the clinic. This meant we had to hire more drivers. In general, we discovered we needed to provide more social services to meet seniors' needs in Virginia than we did in South Florida. One of our first moves was to partner with local churches to help.

The biggest initial problem we faced was getting these new patients to change their habits for seeking healthcare. Before we arrived, it would take at least six months to get in to see a primary care physician, and they were all fee-for-service providers who encouraged patients to go to an emergency room if they needed immediate care rather than come to them. The hospitals would admit them, resulting in around $15,000 in charges to Medicare, the cost of most DRGs—the Diagnosis Related Group of bundled charges typical for most hospital admissions. Our model of value-based care meant JenCare would have to absorb those expenses. We had to train our patients to come to us first, not the emergency room.

"Why do you want to see me so often?" they would ask. "Are you trying to bill Medicare to make more money?"

We would have to explain.

"We don't get paid for seeing you more often. We get paid by getting you healthy and keeping you healthy. By seeing you more often, we can monitor your progress toward good health, and we have more opportunities to get you healthier. We both win!"

Changing their understanding of healthcare from sickness-based to wellness-based and their behavior from going to an emergency room to coming to our center were major challenges in Virginia. And they're ones we've experienced in every new area we've entered.

WE ALSO QUICKLY discovered that our medical costs were much higher than what we had been told by Humana, which required us to adjust our business model. The company simply didn't have enough information to give an accurate assessment of the costs. The patients were new to Humana's system, so it took some time to accumulate the data needed to build a workable business model. The subset of data Humana had was for much healthier patients than those whom we began to serve.

Initially, these five centers incurred massive losses. Each center was burning thousands of dollars a day just to stay open. As one of us said in those early days: "We better grow and we better heal our patients; otherwise, every day we're flushing money down the toilet!" The higher costs for patients who required more specialists and hospitalizations than anticipated, along with the initial multimillion-dollar investment for operating and buildout, meant that we had two strong imperatives to get our patients healthier faster—a clinical imperative because they were sicker than expected and a business imperative because our costs were higher than expected.

We also had to adjust because Virginia's healthcare regulations differed from Florida's. In Virginia, for example, medical assistants could not assist doctors in dispensing medications as they could in Florida. And the regulations for what nurse practitioners could do in the clinics differed as well.

Not only did we find out our patients in Virginia were physically sicker than we'd expected, we also had to address greater behavioral and mental health needs in Virginia than among our Florida patients. Depression, anxiety, substance abuse, and addiction—all are signs of a population that needs to be loved and supported. The preponderance of patients in this area who had served in the military during wartime, and the trauma of that service, may well have contributed to this greater need.

Gordon recalls being on-site just after the Portsmouth center had been completed and opened. A little old lady grabbed his hand. "Thank you so much for coming here," she said. "God bless you! It means so much to us. No one else was coming to help us, and we thank God for you!"

Gordon was deeply touched by her appreciation and sincerity. Our care, focused on patients, their needs, and their wants, was making a powerful difference in people's lives. Stories like hers resonated with all of us. We sensed that God wanted us to continue building on what had prompted Dad and Mom to begin their work in that one clinic in South Florida. We wondered—how many folks around the country are hungry for the same thing?

Our clinics in South Florida grew as our systems became even more finely tuned. We had taken Bob Kocher's advice, nailed down a scalable model with the original five, and now had grown to thirteen centers (eight in Florida, five in Virginia).

Chris's focus was on making sure JenCare's rollout was on point and set up for success, and more of South Florida's growth and clinical culture shifted to Gordon. He and Jessica built the clinical infrastructure needed to support both South Florida's ChenMed centers and JenCare in Virginia, particularly recruiting and training physicians.

Between 2011 and 2014, we experienced even greater

growth. From North Dade County we moved into Broward County, soon expanding ChenMed to twelve clinics in South Florida. In 2012 we added two more JenCare clinics in Virginia, then went into Kentucky and New Orleans, continuing our partnership with Humana. In 2013, JenCare added clinics in Chicago and Atlanta.

While things were quite tight financially as JenCare got off the ground, the operations finally stabilized and these centers became very productive. As our patients got healthier, we were able to simplify their medications and focus more on prevention and wellness. When they had a need, they came to us rather than the ER. Now JenCare is woven deep into the fabric of those communities. It is extremely successful, serving more than fifty thousand seniors who came to us as the poorest and frailest seniors in those areas.

JENCARE IS A joint venture with Humana in five states— Virginia, Kentucky, Louisiana, Illinois, and Georgia. ChenMed operates the business as majority owners. Humana funded most of the expansion on the front end, which in ten years has given them a massive return. ChenMed provides all the "sweat equity" to operate the clinics.

At the time of our deal with Humana, Bruce Perkins, along with their new CEO Bruce Broussard, wanted to establish a national presence and posture for their company. They knew they needed primary care groups that understood how to manage for risk and for value. Broussard's background was in running doctor groups, so he immediately saw the beauty of our model for delivering healthcare. He was fully on board from the beginning. Humana is now the leading plan in every market that JenCare expanded into with them as partners. This was not true when we started together.

As wildly successful as JenCare and our partnership with Humana proved, we eventually realized that it is not a prudent business model on our part to work with only one plan. If patients prefer another plan over Humana, we can't serve them. When we decided to expand into Pennsylvania, we did it with the intent to work with multiple payers outside the JenCare partnership. We needed to be able to accept other payers to get enough patients to make our centers viable and profitable.

It's only logical that other payers would be less willing to send their patients to a center partially owned by Humana. With that knowledge, we grew a new brand, called Dedicated Senior Medical Centers. We did more market research and ventured into other parts of Florida (Lakeland, Jacksonville, Tampa, and West Palm Beach), and from Pennsylvania we moved into Ohio, Tennessee, Texas, Michigan, and Missouri— all under the Dedicated Senior Medical Center brand and all fully owned by ChenMed.

By partnering with multiple payers, we have had much more flexibility and speed. If a plan is available in a state and is willing to work with us, we can do that. We don't need long, drawn-out corporate approvals—we can move quickly so long as the plan is aligned, and we choose good locations where we can grow members.

Seeing how well our model was working, what we call

"Me Too ChenMeds" began sprouting up. In other words, others began to copy our model. We love that! Not only does the competition motivate us to get better, it means that even more patients are getting the hands-on attention and medical care they need to live full, vibrant lives. Many of those who copied us have gone public, with tremendous financial results and results for their members.

Doing the right thing, the right way, really can pay off for everyone.

# CHAPTER 7

# THE CHENMED WAY

WE RECEIVED THIS in an email from one of our newer PCPs in June 2021:

*I interviewed for my position back in October. I was emotionally drained from my clinic job. My husband and I both worked for the same full-risk model company at the time, my patient panel was 2,700, and my two boys (three years old at the time) were in daycare 7:00 a.m. to 6:00 p.m. Monday through Friday. It's not the lifestyle I envisioned, and I was deeply saddened over my job and the fact that I simply was unhappy and felt as if I was not providing the care they deserved.*

*Fast forward to June. I have been with ChenMed for more than sixty days now, and I leave my clinic each day so incredibly happy and fulfilled. I love my job; that's not something I could have said six months ago. I felt the need to let you know, because I hope you realize that you are not just changing the lives of seniors, you are changing the lives of physicians. I have never felt like I had a purpose until now, and I firmly believe I was meant to be here. Thank you not only for giving physicians a place to feel valued with the work that they do, but also for creating such an amazing work family filled with other providers who purely just want to help. I'm truly grateful. Thank you.*

It's been our joy and privilege to see, not only the lives of our seniors, but the lives of our doctors transformed as well. We train our PCPs for success in their practice and their lives using the ChenMed method for practicing medicine, and that training has gone through many changes and improvements over the years.

And those changes and improvements will continue as long as they're necessary.

WITH THE ADDITION of new centers and our expansion into new parts of the country, we needed many more primary care physicians to support our mandate of offering life-improving healthcare to seniors. Finding doctors with the clinical skills to meet that challenge is not terribly difficult. Finding doctors willing to practice medicine using a very different model than the one in which they were trained proved much more so. We quickly realized that hiring someone with a medical degree and a good résumé, giving them a laptop or a tablet, and telling them to go see patients was far from sufficient. Our half day of training in Miami soon became one week, then two weeks, and has now evolved into an intensive four- to six-week training with additional follow-up that can last for two years.

We knew we needed great doctors because of the deteriorating health conditions so many seniors have when they first come to us. But under the standard methodology of healthcare, most physicians are trained to offer transactional healthcare: *I have been trained to transfer the knowledge I have gained to my patient. Once I have done that, we are done.* That doctor is then paid for the number of those transactions she or he performed.

We have designed our care to inspire behavioral change within our patients. We desire better outcomes than merely alleviating symptoms of disease. We want to hear seniors articulate their health goals, give them the tools they need to reach those goals, and then coach them to better health. This requires relationship. We have to find physicians who are willing to learn about behavioral and lifestyle change and how to develop a caring relationship with their patients, and ones who are open and humble enough to consider receiving additional training.

Think about it. You've gone through four years of medical school, a few years of internship and residency, perhaps an additional fellowship, and you're finally licensed and ready to practice medicine on your own. In addition, you're an extremely bright individual who has weathered the challenges of medical school and training and reached "attending" status. Then ChenMed invites you to join our team of physicians, but you're told there will be additional training necessary to practice medicine a new way that requires influence and leadership. Even after recognizing that these qualities—influence, behavior change, and leadership—were not focused on in medical school and training, it still takes a special kind of individual willing to embrace something so different from the status quo. Candidates need to recognize that there are significant limitations to the existing model of care and be willing to continue to learn and adapt to new challenges.

As we expanded from our South Florida clinics to the JenCare centers, we used headhunters to help us find doctors. It didn't take long for us to realize that they were merely a sourcing instrument, simply providing names of potential candidates. It was up to us to do all the in-depth interviews and vetting to bring in only the best PCPs. And by the best, we mean doctors best suited for our patients, for the ChenMed model, and for our organization.

We're less concerned with academic or research credentials and more interested in finding great clinicians who connect with patients and are willing to learn. Would we rather have doctors who are top researchers from the top five medical schools but who are not interested in relationships, or doctors with fewer published articles and shorter résumés but who have higher levels of emotional intelligence and self-awareness? As long as they are great clinicians who are humble and interested in learning to be change agents with their patients, it doesn't matter where they completed their training or the country in which they went to medical school.

Chris describes himself as a prime example of the difference between the training offered by some of the very best schools and programs in the world and the real-world experience gained by providing the loving care to patients using the method our father designed. Chris came out of his training in cardiovascular specialties at Harvard and Cornell with five board certifications. Back in Miami, he saw his first patient, a man who had just come out of the hospital with heart failure.

"I've got this," Chris says he thought to himself. "I examined him, tweaked his meds, and told him to come back for a follow-up in a month. Back in my training, I would have told him to come back in three months. But since Dad's philosophy was to see patients every month, I thought I was doing something better than normal."

That patient went home. Five days later, he was back in the hospital. This time, however, he didn't make it. Chris was stopped at the nurses' station by Jenny Perdermo, who was running our front desk at that time, after she learned about the man's death.

"Dr. Chen, what happened?" she asked.

"What do you mean?" he asked. "It's tragic, of course. But you know this. Patients die."

"Tell me what happened, specifically," she insisted.

"I increased this medication, decreased that one, and told him I would see him in a month," Chris answered.

"Dr. Chen!" she exclaimed. "A month?!"

"Yeah, a month," he said. A bit full of himself at the time, he was thinking, *You know, I really do know what I'm doing!*

"But a month? You really told him to wait and come back in a month?" she remained incredulous, as if she were saying, *Are you kidding me?*

Finally, Chris asked, "OK. What's up?"

"A month is only the starting point, the bare minimum for us," Jenny said. "For our patients who have had heart failure, we start by seeing them every single day to make sure we know how they're doing and that they're OK. Then we go to twice a week for a while, then once a week. Only when we know all is well do we go back to seeing them monthly."

It certainly hurt his pride, with all the letters, diplomas, and accolades he had accumulated. But Chris had the sense to listen and acknowledge that Jenny, not himself, was the one who knew what she was doing.

Since that time, Chris has never had a patient die or be readmitted to the hospital for heart failure. Not once. He's had patients come to him with stage four hospice care heart failure who are still alive more than ten years later. If he had offered them the typical care, statistically those patients would have been dead within six months.

"That's the difference between what my fancy education taught me and what I learned from a front office staff member who understood the ChenMed Core Model long before it was formally spelled out," he says. "I'm so glad she called me out. Here I was, thinking I was so smart. But I was taught how to treat heart failure by a front desk nurse, and thank God! Many people are alive today because of the lesson she gave me."

Jenny has been with ChenMed for more than twenty-five years. She's now our National Hospital Coordinator.

"What I've learned," Chris says, "is that heart failure, which is the leading issue with senior care today, is 90 percent preventable. Ninety percent! And that's not using anything fancy—no special procedure or technology or device or medications. Using generic medications that have been around for twenty to thirty years—your basic bread-and-butter care—this killer is absolutely preventable. The requirement is a healthcare model that puts the patient first, invests the time and energy in earning their trust, and then coaches them through a transition to better habits and health."

WE HAVE AN appropriate acronym now for the type of physician who fits us well—A.L.L. in—which means they are:

Aligned with our mission, vision, and values; have
Learning agility; and
Learning humility.

Our PCPs need to be A.L.L. in. It isn't always true, but we have noticed a trend—the fancier and longer the *curricula vitae,* the less humility we find in the candidate. Humility can be taught—not to all, but to some—and most people who have made it through medical school possess learning agility. But the most important of those elements is for the physician to be aligned with our mission, our vision, and our values. If the doctor doesn't care about seniors, isn't interested in transforming care for the neediest populations, and can't display love, accountability, and passion, then they're really not for us.

This was the beginning of our feedback cycle. We learned from the physicians who were a good fit for us, who adapted and flourished with our methods, and then we fed that knowledge back to the recruiters to help us identify potential doctors. Our recruiters became the first link in the chain of building relationships with physicians and beginning their education in a new model for practicing medicine. That gave us a jump-start on finding future ChenMed physicians—women and men attracted to growth and development, to leadership and influence, who had a heart for helping older, poorer, sicker seniors. Their clinical training, while a baseline, became secondary to the question of whether they had the potential to be A.L.L. in.

After recruiting, our next challenge was how best to train our physicians in the ChenMed method of delivering healthcare, ultimately preparing them to be agents of change.

CHRIS TRAINED the initial twenty-five to thirty physicians in South Florida. Once Gordon and Jessica were full-time, they began taking the reins for the physician training, particularly when JenCare opened in 2011 and Chris focused more on business development. It was one-on-one training—a one-week crash course learning how to practice medicine in a value-based healthcare system. Most of our doctors come from the traditional fee-for-service world. We show them how what we do differs from fee-for-service, why it's a better method of medical practice, and why it allows physicians to practice the way they've always wanted to practice medicine.

We train them in both the original PCP model of influence, relationship building, and full accountability as well as how to use the proprietary electronic medical records technology. Both were originally developed by our dad. The technology allowed our centers to be interconnected across all our regions, which helps our doctors share information and learn from one another.

Not only were our trainees learning from us—we immediately started learning from them. The feedback we received from those first groups let us know that we had crammed too much into one week for it to be successfully applied in their centers. They needed more time to process and assimilate all the information and methods to feel proficient using our model. One week became two weeks of training in Miami. Then we checked back in with our PCPs at four weeks and six weeks, asking follow-up questions.

*What do you know now that you wish had known before you started?*

*What do you wish you had received during the two-week training period?*

*Where did we go into too much detail that was unnecessary for your successful transition to the ChenMed Way?*

We continue to refine and adjust our training to the needs and desires of our doctors. When we realize too much information on any given topic is not helpful in establishing a practice with us and building a patient panel of 400 to 450, some things are condensed. Other areas are expanded to better serve our PCPs and set them up for success.

ONCE YOU'RE AN attending physician, you're at the top of the totem pole. When you were a medical student, you were given more and more responsibility as you progressed through your third and fourth years. Then as an intern, you found yourself back at the bottom. As a resident you move up again, but once you graduate, feedback from mentors typically stops. No one is looking over your shoulder any longer, no one oversees your work.

That's how being a doctor works in the fee-for-service model. No one comes alongside the physician to say, *How can I help you get better?* Attendings are typically too busy and focused on their own practices to mentor anyone else.

At ChenMed, that's totally different. Early on, we asked the question, *How do we know if we as PCPs are giving VIP service to our seniors?* And by VIP service, we don't mean presenting ourselves as a five-star resort or concierge practice. We mean that we have earned our patients' trust through the way we treat them and how we care for them. When this happens, they will call us first when they're not feeling well, rather than going straight to the ER, where they may experience complications or catch something that we could have prevented.

To answer that question, we've specifically done two things. The first is utilizing patient surveys. Feedback from our seniors themselves is critical to learn what we are doing well and what we can do better to earn and keep their trust.

The second is called *facilitated practice*. We developed it from the concepts of deliberate practice, which is based on the idea that practice doesn't make perfect, but *perfect* practice makes perfect. With deliberate practice, targeted improvement opportunities can be identified during the normal practice of medicine.

With facilitated practice, we allow physicians the

opportunity to be coached by other physicians and help each other get better. It involves having another physician join you in the exam room in order to help you get feedback on key areas where you'd like to improve. It's not exactly shadowing, but it does involve another set of eyes, a coach, to offer feedback on specific, targeted areas. You might say that:

Shadowing + Deliberate Practice = Facilitated Practice

One physician observes and coaches based on the interaction between patient and physician. What we see over and over is that our physicians actually learn from each other through facilitated practice. It's true bi-directional learning. A tech-savvy coach may come into the exam room to help the physician engage more efficiently with technology during a patient exam. But the tech-savvy doctor may learn something about providing better VIP service to her own patients by watching the rapport the attending physician has with his patient.

Most often feedback will begin with something along the lines of "Have you thought about trying *xyz*?" Here's an example of possible feedback to improve VIP service:

"Hey, maybe you should let the patient talk a little bit longer before you interrupt. They were saying something important there, and I think you might have missed something."

Or it can be as simple as:

"I was in with Dr. So-and-so the other day, and I saw him do such-and-such. I've incorporated it into my practice, and it really helped! You might want to try it yourself."

As our doctors experience it, they come to realize that facilitated practice helps them make better use of their time professionally and see better results with their patients. This spills over into other areas of their lives.

Over the years, we have developed a whole methodology around facilitated practice. We focus on areas like helping doctors with clinical prioritization—having listened closely to the patient articulate their health goals, what is the best immediate and doable response the doctor should offer for that patient? We've already mentioned incorporating technology and engaging with the patient for VIP service; we also encourage facilitated practice for our PCPs to improve the efficiency and effectiveness when working with their care team.

Every one of us participates in this, not just new PCPs. And it is ongoing. We pick one of the four areas—clinical prioritization, tech savviness, VIP service, or care team management—and we invite another PCP especially gifted in that area to come alongside and offer feedback and help. Every doctor in the ChenMed system uses this at various times in their practice. It's never punitive but always encouraging and intended to build up and strengthen. And it isn't scary—not like a situation in which a boss is looking over the shoulder of a subordinate. Facilitated practice is all about mutuality, of looking for ways in which we can sharpen our skills on our shared journey to success for our patients and success for ourselves. It's similar to the *See One, Do One, Teach One* method of residency training.

Facilitated practice is a critical part of the intentional training we offer one another at ChenMed. We want to be as efficient as possible in our effectiveness. Our goal is for each of our PCPs to see about twenty patients a day. If we can cut one minute of time with those patients through efficiency, without negatively impacting the effectiveness of that time, then that PCP has gained one hundred minutes a week to invest in their team, in growth as a physician, or in some other area of their life (like family!). Over time, saving that one minute per visit can save days, weeks, and months by picking up effectiveness and efficiency tips from those who do it well.

People with a growth mindset have all benefited from using facilitated practice. Seeing how it's beneficial for themselves, they're willing and excited about sharing it with others. We've cultivated that culture—it's only beneficial to you *if* you want to get better, if you want to be more efficient. *Do you want to finish by 5:00 p.m.* and *deliver great outcomes for your patients? Let's explore together ways to help you win both personally and professionally.*

If we're honest, most of us have that streak of "what's in it for me" inside. Facilitated practice profits everyone who is willing to participate in it. Have all our doctors arrived at this point? No, a few who came to us with more experience found it harder to accept. But almost everyone credits facilitated practice as being a major contributor to their success.

At ChenMed, we work hard at creating a learning environment of openness, discovery, and teamwork. We look to tear down artificial barriers around physicians. No one of us is on a pedestal—every team member is to be respected and honored. We recognize that this is highly unusual in the medical field. We're breaking the mold. By possessing a deliberate, open, curious mindset going in and while getting feedback, everyone wins in the end.

A FEW YEARS AGO we introduced a new method of training for all of our PCPs—"Case-Based Learning." We integrate all learning into clinical cases. Using the treatment of diabetes as an example, here's how it works. Diabetes is a major source of health issues for seniors, so PCPs already knew the clinical treatment of this disease when they joined our team. But we also need to ensure they identify and correctly document any complications early to prevent progression to blindness, kidney disease, or amputations, as well as address the underlying life-style factors that can fuel progression—like what they eat and how much they exercise. Most medical schools have very little education on nutrition and how to motivate behavior change on diet and lifestyle. We include it in our training.

Our PCPs also needed to be aware of the quality-of-care measures for patients with diabetes and ensure they are addressed at the right time. Lastly, PCPs required instruction on the value-based approach to managing diabetes and how to dig deeper to understand why patients may not be adhering to a treatment plan—is it that they can't afford a co-pay, or they have a side effect they didn't want to bother their doctor with? Are they embarrassed to admit they can only afford fast food or what they get from the food bank? In private practice, using the fee-for-service model, doctors never had to deal with that.

A patient once gave an example of the care they received before joining ChenMed: "The doctor told me, 'You have diabetes. I need you to lose weight; take these two medications and I'll see you again *in six months.*'" At ChenMed, we help our PCPs learn to explore the root causes of diabetes and ways to reverse the disease with each patient, even as we treat the symptoms. Through case-based learning, our PCPs learn the best medicines to use as alternatives.

It's really a back-to-basics approach. From a clinical perspective, we want our PCPs prepared to identify comorbidities they need to address and to prevent the long-term complications of diseases like diabetes. As opposed to separate modules for various organs and health conditions, we integrate all aspects of organ systems and conditions into one module using case-based learning.

JUST AS THE RAPID addition of new centers required scalability in our systems and methods, the need for more PCPs to serve in those centers required scalability of our recruiting and training as well.

Scalability makes it meaningful and durable—it can't be a one-off. We had to identify scalable ways to change patient behaviors in an affordable way and scalable ways to serve seniors with VIP care that delivers better health results.

We realized that you can't get to better health without changing behavior. You can't change behavior without having influence. As best-selling author and leadership guru John Maxwell has said, "Leadership is influence, nothing more, nothing less." Most physicians typically rely on the most basic form of influence—their degree and their credentials. While that is necessary, it isn't sufficient. To truly drive more influence, doctors need to learn more about themselves and their patients. Our PCPs had to be able to build relationships with their patients and connect with them on a deeper level. We want to demonstrate greater outcomes for our seniors and teach others to do the same. Thus, the necessity for a system to mass-produce these physician/leaders, these agents or champions of change.

It doesn't take much influence for a doctor to change a medicine—they simply write a new prescription. But if that doctor wants their patient to change their diet; to change their exercise routine; to change and become an active participant engaged in their own healthcare; to change how often they proactively seek care; to change by focusing on prevention of issues rather than a simple reactive approach, then that doctor requires much more than their credentials to achieve that level of change.

Which brings us back to relationships. It's a call to close, personal, human interaction, in which the PCP listens to the patient articulate their health goals. We dive deep into a concept called motivational interviewing, and all of our PCPs receive extensive training in applying its techniques. What are the motivators the patient already holds that will inspire them to change? How can we help our patients articulate their own motivators? Once the doctor hears and understands those, then they can coach the patient through the steps to achieving better health.

Here are several examples of how this works. As we share these stories, keep in mind that there are thousands of these, because all of our PCPs are doing this on a daily basis.

A physician friend Gordon trained with called to ask for

advice and help with his father. The dad, who was seventy-four years old at the time, was on a heart transplant list, suffering from irretractable chest pain. He was on eight medications. If he walked at all, he felt tremendous pressure in his chest and would have to sit down and rest. He had gotten to the point that the medications were no longer effective. After already having bypass surgery and multiple stents put in, the surgeons would no longer operate on him—they told him he needed a different heart.

Because he knew Gordon and his reputation through his son, the father and Gordon immediately experienced a good rapport. Still, Gordon needed to build trust and develop their relationship. He recommended a book that encouraged a change in diet to improve heart health. They discussed it at an appointment, and Gordon asked if he was willing to make a change. "I know that changing your diet can be difficult," he said. "But making this change is no more dramatic than having a heart transplant!"

They laughed together at the comparison. The dad changed to a whole food, plant-based diet from a diet dominated by animal products. In the United States, most animal products have an inflammatory impact on the body. The animals are injected with hormones and steroids for mass production. Farmers take shortcuts to increase volume and profitability. Also, the conditions many animals are raised in increase the rates of infection in the meat we eat. Americans, by and large, ingest horrendous food, which causes plaque to develop in the blood vessel walls.

The friend's dad also cut out cheese, which is the number one source of saturated fats. By making a dramatic change in his diet, he experienced dramatic results. Over a period of three to six months, while seeing both Gordon and his primary care physician—another ChenMed clinician—they were able to take him off four of his medications and off the transplant list. His chest pain was gone. He was able to walk and travel again. Doing something as simple as changing his diet changed his life. Gordon served as an agent of change, monitoring his transition from heavy medications and heart pain to an improved quality and longer life.

Chris had a patient in her sixties, a woman with class four (or end stage) heart failure. She was around five feet, six inches tall and weighed somewhere between three hundred to four hundred pounds. Chris was seeing her every week, knowing that statistics tell us that half of those patients will die within six months. In her condition, she actually qualified for hospice. After two months of refining her medications, he knew he needed to do more. He decided to address her diet.

"What do you eat for breakfast?" he asked.

"A piece of toast," she replied.

Chris was thinking, *Half a loaf? A full loaf?* But he asked, "Just one?"

"Oh, yes. Just one. I'll put a bit of butter and jelly on it. But just one."

"OK," he said. "How about for lunch?"

"A bowl of soup," she quickly replied. "Usually chicken soup. It's my favorite. And I may have one piece of bread with that."

Chris was running out of meals. He figured the culprit

had to be dinner.

"OK. So how about dinner? What do you eat then?"

"Either turkey or chicken," she said.

"How much turkey or chicken?"

"Oh, a few slices of turkey, or a thigh and a leg of chicken."

Chris was really starting to wonder about this. But he kept probing. He was thinking at this point, maybe two bowls of mashed potatoes.

"What else do you have with your turkey or chicken?"

"A small amount of corn, usually. And another piece of bread."

This was making no sense to Chris. The number of calories she was describing did not add up for the size of this woman. He decided to interview her daughter, who agreed to come in with her mom to talk with him. The daughter was extremely appreciative of the interest and care Chris was offering, telling him he was the first doctor who truly seemed to care about her mom. Then the daughter took the initiative.

"Dr. Chen, I need your help," she said.

"Sure, I'll do whatever I can," he said.

"I need you to talk to my mom and tell her that eating an entire bucket of fried chicken every night at midnight is really bad for her health."

Chris looked at the mom in astonishment.

"What? What happened here? You didn't say anything about this when we talked about your diet."

"Well," the mom answered, "you never asked me what I ate at midnight."

171

Chris was able to convince the mom to cut out the fried chicken. Over the next year and a half, she lost around 150 pounds. She went from impending death within six months to being healthy with another fifteen years of life, easily. It wasn't pills, procedures, or surgeries that made her better. It didn't take a fifty-thousand-dollar hospital visit to make her better. All it took was caring, changing her diet, getting her to walk every day once her heart was strong enough, and then the pounds peeled away and her good health returned.

Today in medicine doctors are trained to spend, and they prefer to spend, hundreds of thousands of dollars in procedures. For this woman, it took eight twenty-minute sessions over an eight-week period to discover that the real culprit was a bucket of fried chicken. Ask just about anyone, and we're pretty confident they will say that an investment of two hours and forty minutes is well worth it to add ten to twenty years of life, along with the added benefit of *not* spending hundreds of thousands of dollars on medical care!

Our current system doesn't think of healthcare correctly. Eighty percent of a person's health is determined not by what is learned or talked about in medical school. It is genetics along with lifestyle and behaviors, plus overcoming educational, safety, environmental, and food insecurity barriers to good care.

Some medical practitioners take the approach of "if the patient wants to die, let them die." With this patient, Chris took a much more assertive approach. Because he had earned the trust of the patient and her family, as well as getting to know their family situation, he was able to take a stronger stance with her. With some patients, a doctor may be able to take more of a partnership approach. It requires that consistent time, asking the right questions, and listening to the patient to know which approach is best for that person.

Here's another example: Gordon was participating in a facilitated practice with a new PCP in Lakeland, Florida. The doctor was struggling with how to influence her patients to come in more than twice a year. Gordon went in with her to see a new patient.

"I'm pretty healthy," the patient began. "I've been on these five medications for a few years now. I really don't need to come in monthly. My diabetes and high blood pressure seem to be under control."

Gordon asked the PCP and the patient for permission to talk.

"How long do you want to live?" he asked the patient.

She was seventy-eight at the time.

"I'd like to live to a hundred," she said.

"OK," he said as he noted that. "How do you want to function in your life? Would you like to get off medications? Maybe lose some weight?"

The patient agreed that she would like to get off medications and lose some weight.

"That's achievable," Gordon said. "But to do that we may need to change a few things. First, we're going to make sure your medications are appropriate for where you are health-wise right now. As we monitor your progress, we can hopefully get you off some of them. You may not need to be on blood pressure and diabetes medicine for the next twenty-two years. Would you like that?"

"Sure!" she agreed.

"Do you think you could walk at least a mile a day?"

She nodded affirmatively.

"If we're going to get you to a hundred years old, then we eventually want to aim for three miles a day. Our research shows that is doable for someone just like you."

The patient smiled and nodded again.

"Now, here's what we need to do to get you there. Your doctor needs to be able to check how you're doing, to help you develop and keep these habits that will help you live longer and better. We want to make sure they're sticking, right?"

More agreement from the patient.

"And if you have any questions along the way, any at all, we'll be here and available to answer them and help. Especially as you're able to increase your exercise, and as we're able to pull back on some of these meds, we want to make sure you're doing OK. To do that, we need to see you at least once every month. Is that OK with you?"

"Absolutely!" the patient said.

That's what happens when we focus on the patient's goals compared to only the doctor's goals! The new PCP saw that the relationship is more about helping her patient achieve her goals than getting the patient to achieve the physician's goals.

The PCP is there to help seniors change their behaviors, but it starts with trust, influence, and coaching.

Patients expect their PCPs to know their history, to be

up-to-date on their conditions, and to advocate for them. To do that effectively requires investing in and developing the relationship so that trust is earned. Only then can you speak to their lives and influence behavioral change as their health coach. Once that happens, they're usually willing and eager to come back for monthly check-ins.

MOST PHYSICIANS don't have an awareness that this world of influence exists. They're not trained in it in medical school or in residency. Most physicians focus on memorizing articles, chapters, anatomy, physiology—but not self-discovery. They don't have time for it. Medical students never feel like they have enough time to study for a test, much less dig into self-discovery and how they can influence others. You can always spend another hour or two studying for that next test, but it's hard to rationalize carving out time for your own self-development, growth, and discovery. Those muscles atrophy and become weak. They need an awakening.

Our PCP training at ChenMed is geared to help our physicians get stronger in openness, in vulnerability, in curiosity. Then they can serve as change agents. We've developed a process that doesn't just focus on making our PCPs better doctors—they're in the process of becoming better human beings. We work on caring *about*, not just caring *for*, our patients. When we go into communities as change agents for individual patients, we become change agents for the entire community.

Our training produces better communicators, better listeners, and doctors who possess better interpersonal skills.

That not only helps them to be successful at ChenMed—it helps them succeed in their marriages, with their kids, and with their friends.

During our recruiting, it's critical that we get the "who" right. We want to attract and retain PCPs who love and thrive in what we do, who love taking care of seniors, who love learning humility, learning agility, learning new things, and who love making a difference.

As with many things, the 80/20 rule applies. When we select well, 80 percent of the work is behind us. When we select poorly, 80 percent of the work is ahead of us. That's why a lot of our focus is on choosing the right PCPs.

Jessica does a lot of work now with our training.

"It's so much fun watching them mature and evolve," she says. "Watching them grow their panel, watching them make a huge difference in their patients' lives and in their own—it's so rewarding. I have so many come back after a few months with us and tell me that making the transition to ChenMed was the best decision they've ever made."

As we've grown, we've brought in a very diverse group of physicians. It's not just one type of doctor who has a heart for the communities we serve. We have every race and culture represented on our team. We have more physician diversity than most organizations—our physicians tell us they feel comfortable in our model and environment, and they appreciate our mission to make a difference in poor, underserved communities. We also have more women than men, a trend we're seeing in healthcare in general.

We've also had top physician leaders in other organizations join us as practicing PCPs on a leadership development track. Among them are Dr. Danny Guerra, who was a prior associate chief medical information officer at a large health system, and Dr. Faisel Syed, a former chief medical officer of one of the country's largest federally qualified health centers. Here at ChenMed, Dr. Guerra now leads our medical informatics nationally, and Dr. Syed has progressed from a practicing PCP to serving as national director of primary care. In 2021 he had the opportunity to present our ChenMed model before the United States Congress. The trust physician leaders place in us is critical, and we take their growth and development very seriously. Ours is a model where top clinical leaders attract other top clinical leaders in a mission-driven and family culture of fulfilling purpose and personal opportunity.

That's the type of organization ChenMed has become. Our physician culture is one of the most important keys for ChenMed to be effective at accomplishing our mission, fulfilling our vision, and continuing to produce fruit from our values. As we do that, hundreds of thousands of lives are impacted for the better.

# CHAPTER 8

# FAMILY MATTERS

WE FIND IT especially interesting that ChenMed was growing exponentially during a major financial crisis. The housing and financial markets were in deep trouble after the 2008 market crash. By God's mercy and grace, combined with the diversity of gifts and talents in our family, we have been able to accomplish what God has called us to do.

Chris's great strength is looking outside healthcare to identify what we can learn from other industries and organizations. He is keenly attuned to finding opportunities for growth and can think broadly and quickly to identify them. As he likes to say, he's a businessman who happens to be a doctor.

To discover how to scale healthcare, we couldn't find the answer in healthcare because no one else was doing it. Chris met with the CEO of Interstate Batteries at the time, Carlos Sepulveda, and Carlos became one of his mentors. He met with the people who coached the owners of Chick-fil-A through their growth. Chris developed a strong relationship with Horst Schulze, founder of Ritz-Carlton, who now serves on our board of directors. By meeting with McKinsey consultants Bob Kocher and Todd Johnson, he studied how McKinsey successfully scaled culture, infusing its vision, values, and behaviors consistently across every aspect of the organization. He brought in people from these other industries to meet with our family and leadership team.

"Every one of us has a role here," Chris says. "Dad created the ChenMed system. When I came on board, I realized that my job was to make Dad's dream a reality. He was the inventor of health-care transformation. My responsibility was to make that transformation scalable, so we could offer our services in hundreds if not thousands of locations. Together we've taken his dream and turned it into a vision that others could follow, a mission that others could deliver. I recognize that I am not the most talented member of our family, with one area that I excel in. My contribution and passion are to combine the amazing talents and contributions of our people, helping them work as a unit to build a system that fulfills our mission and vision for healthcare."

Gordon's strength is more internally focused, inspiring and developing our center leaders and physicians to understand and work within the ChenMed model, working cross-functionally and executing our core model at scale. He's a physician who happens to be a businessman. When speaking to physicians, Gordon helps them realize the vision and understand what it will mean to them and their practice to provide care within the ChenMed system.

Chris says, "No one can talk with doctors and share our vision for changing healthcare like Gordon can. No one! He inspires doctors to leave the fee-for-service matrix. Standing firmly on his values, he leads the troops in the revolution."

Mom's strength is administration, running the business side of healthcare, overseeing our operations and buildings. She brings a discipline and strength that is unparalleled and a business tenacity that adds balance to the organization. Dad's strength, besides his most important contribution of developing the original model of wellness, value-based healthcare, is compiling and analyzing the data, as well as making sure we're always on the cutting edge with our technology. Dad has a digital mind and thinks in automation and technology. He brings the physician, patient, and business perspective together to help our data become actionable.

Jessica works closely with Gordon, identifying talented doctors and continuing to develop our physicians and physician leaders. She offers tremendous support, training, and wellness programs to help our clinical teams thrive within our model in order to address the burdens of the neediest patients in America.

Stephanie heads up ChenMed's culture team and infuses our values into each one of our centers along with applying her expertise on the legal side. She is the heart and the fun of the organization and helps us achieve nationally recognized awards such as "Great Place to Work!" She creates a sense of purpose and belonging for all team members.

Of course, despite all these unique strengths, there's always complexity in family dynamics. Ours has strong personalities, egos, insecurities, and sensitivities. Receiving feedback from your parents, siblings, or in-laws comes with great challenges. In fact, most people would run away from a similar environment!

Not only that, but what we have to offer one another is not light feedback. Each one of us is totally invested in this endeavor—it is our life's work. So even constructive reviews are deep and personal, and they can literally mean life or death for our patients. We are convinced that we can only survive in the environment God has placed us in with the love of Christ operating among us. We're constantly reminded: it's not about us.

ChenMed's success would not, could not have happened, without God's mercy and grace on our family. Even with our faith in Christ, it's a daily struggle. We challenge one another often to self-assess how we're doing.

"Is my ego flaring up? Oh, it is. Help us, Lord, not to get in our own way and prevent us from being a part of something so beautiful."

We're told, "Be patient, bearing with one another in love" (Ephesians 4:2).

That is no simple or easy task. In fact, it is very, very difficult.

Dad has always said that we are six pieces who fit together into something special to be used by God in mighty ways. Each one different, but all complementary—we're successful because each person is allowed to focus on and be successful in their own area of expertise. We work together as one unified team to accomplish God's purposes for us.

Furthermore, we have amazing and talented executives, business and clinical leaders, and team members who see what God is doing through our family and ChenMed. They have personally seen the love and healing we can bring into so many communities in need and are inspired to join us. They, too, are called to this vision of what healthcare can be and how we collectively can help make it right. We believe it's a spiritual law of the universe, much like the physical law of gravity— when we work together, complementing one another's gifts, the impact of what we can offer our patients is much, much greater than what any one of us could do individually.

As WITH PRETTY much everything that makes us who we are, the intentionality of putting faith and family first begins with Mom and Dad. An example of how that specifically plays out took place the day Chris and Stephanie returned from their honeymoon. Dad greeted Stephanie with a big hug and these words:

"Stephanie, we are thrilled to have you in our family. I would be honored and so happy if you would call me Diddi."

That is so Dad. You see his personality, his humility, his love in welcoming her in that way. Stephanie was nineteen at the time. Wanting to remain respectful, she continued to call Mom "Mrs. Chen" several times that day. Here's how Mom handled that: "Stephanie! Listen to me. You have one week to get used to calling me Mommi. One week! Do you understand?!"

That is so Mom. Direct. Decisive. Demanding. But endearing as well, because she made it clear that her intent was to embrace Stephanie as more than a daughter-in-law. In their own ways, both Mom and Dad let Stephanie know she was the daughter they never had.

Jessica's experience was only slightly different. As she and Gordon were walking out of the church after their wedding—and remember, this was minutes after we found out Dad would be heading to Houston for what we hoped would be a healing treatment of his cancer—Mom stopped her.

"Jessica, now you call me Mommi."

Dad was standing right beside Mom.

"And please call me Diddi."

Mom then added one of her infamous lines to Jessica.

"One more thing. Now you are responsible for all of Gordon's food."

With Stephanie serving as a prime example of what it meant to be embraced as a Chen daughter, Jessica understood immediately what that meant. Both of our wives have never felt that their relationships with Mommi and Diddi in any way diminish or devalue the amazing, loving relationships they have with their own parents. As Stephanie says: "It just adds two people who care about me, who are willing to invest in me, who love me deeply. Why wouldn't I want that in my life?"

Stephanie also describes how she has never been allowed to talk to Chris about "your family" or say "you guys did something great" when talking among the six adults.

"It's always, 'No, Stephanie. It's not my family. It's *our* family' or, 'No. *We* did something great. You are as much a part of us as anyone else.'"

Mom and Dad's intentionality to embrace our wives as equal members of our family effectively broke down barriers and avoided typical in-law issues that so many families have and struggle with.

Here's another example of Mom's love, generosity, and wisdom in nurturing relationships. When both of our wives had very young kids, Mom would call them on a Saturday, oftentimes doing this every other week or so.

"Do you want to go to the mall? Get Chris (or Gordon) to watch the babies. Let's go shopping!" She always took both Stephanie and Jessica together. Never one or the other. The girls would come home with huge bags of clothes that Mom insisted on buying for them. "You need this for work." Or, "This will look so beautiful on you!"

Mom has always been very intentional—she never wanted to be the source of competition or jealousy between the daughters. There are countless other stories of her extreme generosity.

"I found a lady who does manicures in the home." This conversation took place over the phone with Stephanie. "I'll send her to your house when she finishes with me."

While Stephanie enjoys cooking, Jessica doesn't as much, and her work schedule makes organizing meals difficult at times. Rosa, who is much more than a housekeeper or cook for our family, has been an important person in our lives for well over a decade. She's such a fixture in Mom and Dad's kitchen that one of Gordon and Jessica's kids asked one night if they were going to Rosa's house for dinner. When Mom found out how much Jessica loves Rosa's cooking, she started having Rosa cook meals at least once or twice a week and take them over for Gordon and Jessica's family. Mom is always doing little things to say, "I love you." She gets a hard rap for being tough, and deservedly so. But within that tough exterior is one of the kindest, most thoughtful, and generous people you will ever meet—in her own very special way.

"Mommi is the kind of mother-in-law I want to be," Stephanie says. "I want my sons' wives to say, like me, 'Why wouldn't I want to hang out with you for Christmas, or summer vacation, or free time on a Saturday?' I'm loved beyond words. This is definitely as much my family as the one I grew up in."

WE'RE OFTEN ASKED—*How do you do it?* Keep in mind that we don't just work together—with our offices side by side at our headquarters, where we overlap on work teams with one another. We also vacation together and live on the same street! There are three Chen houses right in a row, lot line to lot line to lot line. In fact, we're now in the second neighborhood where we live next door to one another. It's not haphazard or coincidental. We plan to be involved intimately in one another's lives, to make sure we're not just business associates who happen to be in the same family, but a family who works, prays, and plays together.

We recognize that what we have is a unique family dynamic. Very, very few, if any that we know of, can pull this type of closeness off. And it doesn't come easily. We are six type A personalities with strong opinions and individual drives for success. There are moments during the "violent agreements" that erupt from time to time that it sounds like World War III. Those typically occur either between the two of us or between one of us and Mom. If Dad is involved, everyone knows it is very serious. Stephanie says that in the twenty years she's been a part of the family, she can only recall three or four occasions in which Dad has had a major issue with something. She and Jessica have made a conscious choice not to participate in any of these disagreements—they allow the four original Chens to hash things out.

Over the years, we have brought in external consultants and added members to our executive team. They all have taken note of how quickly things can resolve when one of our eruptions takes place.

In the heat of the moment, one of us will interject: "Would God be happy with how this is happening? Would this make God sad?"

From battle lines drawn, it will almost immediately transform into confession, apology, and grace. Confession and apology from the one who escalated the conflict and grace and an offering of peace from the primary recipient of the ire. The atmosphere in the room changes completely.

It's a powerful reality in our Chen family when the offender says, "I'm really sorry. I know that was disgusting. Please. Let's pray." And we do.

This works for us because we all know this is not something we could have done on our own. God is inspiring and blessing our work. Stephanie offers this analogy:

AN UNEDUCATED, talentless individual wins the lottery and then becomes a snob, cutting themselves off from family and old friends. That person did nothing to earn or deserve their change in life. It simply happened to and for them.

We would be that person if we didn't recognize that without God's blessings we are nothing special. That isn't a fake humility—we know it's true. There are probably millions of people in the world who work harder than us, who are smarter than us, who are more talented than us. It is when our egos rise up, when we allow our pride to take front and center stage, that we start to argue. When reminded of that, we stop and thank God for the blessing He has given us, allowing us to do what we do together.

THERE'S AN ADAGE from Jewish wisdom literature that speaks to this truth—"One may be overpowered, and two may stand. But a cord of three strands is not easily broken" (Ecclesiastes 4:12). Our three families are those three strands. Individually, we would be nothing compared to what we are when we allow God to weave and intertwine us with one another. Every one of us, deep in our souls, believes that it is only by the grace of God that we are doing what we are doing today.

It works for us because everyone *wants* in, and everyone is *all* in. We each prioritize our living, working, and having fun together as family. Even when we disagree, we hold to this truth—we're all out for the same thing, we're all here for the right reasons, and we're all going after the same mission, vision, and values. That is intentional—it doesn't come easily all the time, and it requires making a conscious decision to think and live this way. For us, it works—and we believe it can for others.

JESSICA JOKES that when there's a family get-together involving all fourteen of us, she knows she will be able to sit back and relax—she couldn't get a word in even if she wanted to. Mom, Chris, Gordon, and Stephanie are all on the extreme spectrum of extroverts, while Jessica and Dad are the opposite as introverts. What we've learned is that having a wide range of individuals who are willing and eager to work together and cooperate with one another is one of the most important dynamics leading to our success. Jessica puts it this way: "We now have a better understanding of one another's strengths and opportunities. We actively seek to provide one another room to exercise our strengths, and we recognize the opportunities for growth we each have. Especially because of that second part, we're able to cover for one another while we seek to work on our opportunities."

It's significant that Jessica doesn't distinguish between *strengths* and *weaknesses* but *strengths* and *opportunities*. We all now believe that a score in a certain area of Myers-Briggs, or the Enneagram, or DISC, or any other personality evaluation tools cannot be used as an excuse for poor behavior or performance. "Sorry, that's just me" or, "God made me this way, and you'll have to learn to deal with it" doesn't cut it for a Chen. Any given score is merely a base, a starting point that we can work on and develop. Our innate traits are like muscles—they require focused conditioning and intentional concentration. We refuse to make excuses for ourselves or one another. And when we embrace and cooperate with one another's differences, the results are always better than if we went it alone.

Stephanie observed one of the "violent agreements" that the two of us were engaged in. "Guys!" she said. "You're really saying the exact same thing! Chris, you're approaching it from thirty thousand feet in the air. You can't be bothered with what's happening on the ground. 'Don't bog me down with the details!' Gordon, you're focused on the path right in front of you, trying to figure out how you can get to where you both want to be. 'I have to know the details before I can make any progress at all!' The two of you are not in conflict. You're both approaching this opportunity with your own way to make it work. Work together, and I know we will get there."

What we've learned is that our systems, as important as it is to have them, are never perfect. Gordon is able to identify the imperfections in the system, identify things that fall outside the system, and encourage us to establish a new and better system and order. That process can be messy, but only temporarily. It's vitally important not to maintain the system for the system's sake—the system has to serve the mission and the vision. If there's a better way to serve the mission and vision, then it's time to change the system.

Yes, this is another source of friction between us. But that friction produces a better result. King Solomon is rightly lauded for his wisdom when he said, "Iron sharpens iron, and one man sharpens another" (Proverbs 27:17). That is certainly true for the two of us. Chris establishes a system. Gordon then fine-tunes that system over time.

THREE OR FOUR years ago, Chris decided to bring in several consultants from Ronald Blue, a faith-based financial consulting firm, to help us work on our family dynamics. He saw other family businesses falter or fail because they had no one from the outside observing the way they dealt with issues—no one was telling them the truth. With Ronald Blue's help, we learned to distinguish between the business of our family and our family business. By paying attention to and working on our interpersonal relationships, the business of our family, we have become even more effective in our cooperative efforts for ChenMed, the family business. We began to be even more intentional investing in one another outside of our work environment and our roles in ChenMed. Ronald Blue guided us through writing our family mission statement.

We started going on meaningful family trips with our kids, such as to Martin Luther King Jr.'s house in Atlanta and to the Statue of Liberty and Ellis Island to learn about the immigrant experience. We told our kids the Chen family story there.

We now have something like a Jewish bar or bat mitzvah for our children when they reach their twelfth birthday, what we call a "Chen mitzvah." It's a rite of passage as they begin the transition from childhood into a time of increased responsibility. While none of our kids will be required to continue in the family business, they all are brought in to see the importance of the work we do and the many different ways they can be a part of it. Gordon jokes with his kids: "You can be anything you want to be and do anything you want to do. *After* you finish medical school."

With the full support of our wives, we've taken to heart Mom's advice about keeping expectations high for our children. It's not that we expect anything beyond their capabilities, but we do expect them to reach their full potential, and we work hard to give them every opportunity to do just that.

Stephanie and Chris often tell their kids, "We would love for one of you to cure cancer," or, "We would love for one of you to create your own model for underserved kids." When we look at one of our kids and say, "I think you should be the president of the United States," we don't smile when we say it. We mean it. By keeping expectations high for our children, we're communicating to them that they need to prepare themselves for the highest calling God may have on their lives.

Early on, we weren't so good at keeping a good work/life balance. Then we instigated a rule for family vacations that has become one of our favorites—for the first three days we're away, we cannot talk about work. Our nuclear families now spend more time with one another, taking time to reset and focus on individual relationships. As couples, we reconnect as husband and wife. What we've discovered is that our work discussions, when they do happen, are calmer as a result. We're able to have a clearer perspective on work-related topics when we put our families first.

Chris and Stephanie began to take time away for just their family of six—two sons and two daughters. Gordon and Jessica followed suit with their three boys and a girl. The benefits were immediately evident. We could tell a difference and see the appreciation in our interactions with our kids. As couples, we have both instituted a Sabbath rest with our wives —from Friday evening to Saturday evening for Gordon and Jessica, and from Saturday night to Sunday night for Chris and Stephanie; there's no work talk, no email, no phone calls. It's protected time to build into our families.

One of the best pieces of advice both of us have ever received was from our pastor, Dr. Larry Thompson, concerning our relationships with our wives. Marriage, like any critical relationship, needs consistent, recurring investment. It's very simply stated as the three Ds—Dialogue daily, Date weekly, and Depart annually. He helped us understand that the life-long covenant promise we made to our wives was before God. The three Ds were a minimal commitment to fulfill that covenant promise. So every day we connect one-on-one, without devices, and go for a walk. Every week, we try to go out on a dinner date, just husband and wife. And every year, we leave the kids and the rest of the family behind, and we each go somewhere special, just husband and wife.

BEFORE OUR WORK with Ronald Blue, the six adults would meet during the week after hours or on weekends to talk about business. Now we schedule family business meetings during weekday work hours. When we all vacation together, someone may have an "urgent" business matter arise that they want us to address together. But if any of us has something already scheduled with our kids, we've learned to set boundaries.

"Sorry. We told the kids we were going to do *abc*. When

we get back at 6:00 p.m., we can meet from 6:00 to 8:00 p.m. to discuss *xyz*."

To highlight the need for boundaries, Chris tells the story of what happened on one of our family vacations. We were all just getting settled in, and he was in the bathroom. Suddenly he heard a banging on the door. It wasn't a child who needed to go badly. It was Mom.

"Chris, you haven't made a decision about [whatever the urgent business matter was at the time]. You have to make a decision! What are you going to do?"

This episode, and others like it, led all of us to see the wisdom in Ronald Blue's recommendation of appropriate boundaries for us. Our vacations and our lives have a much better work/life balance in them as a result. For Chris, especially, this has been extremely healthy and helpful. Dealing with the pressures of being the CEO of ChenMed nonstop, 24/7 was not sustainable.

WE ARE ALSO BLESSED to have an executive team with members not in the family but who love us and support us as though they are. None of them ever "stirs the pot" for their own advantage. They are all pulling for us and helping us.

Mike Redmond, our Chief Financial Officer, joined that team early on. He's had a front-row seat to observe firsthand how we Chens interact with one another, especially under pressure. A couple of years ago, the pressures of being Chief Executive Officer and all the stress that comes with that were taking a toll on Chris's health. He carries the weight of the company on his shoulders, giving 130 percent of himself to his work. We've learned that excessive stress can be even more poisonous than excessive alcohol on a human body. Mike asked Stephanie, who was serving as our chief in-house legal counsel, to meet with him.

"Stephanie, I don't want to overstep any boundaries here. I love what you're doing for us as our chief legal officer. You've built an awesome team. But"—and he paused before continuing—"may I tell you what I'm thinking?"

"Sure, Mike," she said, with perhaps a bit of trepidation.

"Here's the deal. We can hire other people to do the legal work you're doing for ChenMed. But only you can take care of Chris. I'm really concerned about his health."

Stephanie could have ripped Mike's head off. Most people would agree that she had every right to say something such as, "Who do you think you are to talk about our marriage? And who are you to tell me to take a backseat to my husband and relinquish my career?"

But she didn't. They went on to have what turned out to be a life-changing conversation. Mike went out on a limb to do that because he loves us and our family enough to take that risk. And we had set up an environment in which he felt like he had the freedom to do so. In talking about that conversation and what came out of it, Stephanie says, "I realized that I can be an attorney for the rest of my life. But when we had that conversation, Chris and I had eight more years with our kids in the house, and I had a husband who was coming down with way too many sicknesses and problems for a normally strong and healthy forty-one-year-old."

Chris had just recently undergone cataract surgery and treatment for an ulcer. We had several executive team meetings to discuss the possibility of a change in responsibilities for Stephanie. She then made the switch to serve as our culture officer.

"I no longer get that 9:00 a.m. call telling me that someone has stolen our CDC immunization cards," she says with a twinkle in her eyes. "I'm not the one to call the police and deal with filing federal claims. Now my stress is, 'How can we become and remain a great place to work for all our employees and a great place to visit for our patients?'"

Another member of our executive team had this great idea: during one of our meetings, we hung poster boards with the names of each person on the team. Everyone had different-colored Post-it Notes. We took five minutes of quiet to focus on one person, write something we love and admire about that person, and then put it on their poster. We still hear positive comments about how meaningful that was for team members individually and for us as a unit.

As WE STARTED to grow, Chris studied a number of family companies. Too many get to a certain point and stop growing. They may be good, and even big—but it's unusual for them to reach national prominence. Why? They are an echo chamber. Family members come together and tell one another how amazing they are, convincing one another that they have special blood like a royal family. Chris shared his findings with the rest of us.

"I don't want to hear why we're great," he said. "That's where families fail. As a family, every one of us is deeply committed to one another and to our mission. We all know that. But we cannot do this alone. Let's make that a huge difference between us and other family businesses. Let's hire the best and the brightest to help us fulfill our mission."

We paid way above the norm to get that talent, and our parents let Chris do it. They get the credit for allowing Chris to incorporate this into the culture and vision of our company. When we had only five centers, we hired Federico Cerdeiro, a McKinsey financial guy and MBA graduate of The Wharton School of the University of Pennsylvania, as Chief Business Development Officer. Federico was the first hire to work for us in a high-level business management position. He provided a fresh and incredibly helpful perspective as a thought partner for us in our early days as business leaders. It was a huge investment to propel the business forward because of his business and finance expertise. Then we hired Marke Dickinson, Harvard MBA and former head of marketing for AAA, as Chief Marketing Officer, and Jason Barker, former president of CareMore Health Plans, as our Chief Operating Officer. We adopted the philosophy of taking 80 percent from the best available practices across any industry and then innovating the remaining 20 percent to best suit ChenMed's mission and values.

Family businesses make mistakes by trying to invent everything from scratch, thinking they can do it all. We admit it—we made that mistake in the past. But no more.

Now we learn from others' best practices and tweak it to make it our own.

We hired Adrian Garcia as Controller, who told us we needed to know what we would make in a year and how we would spend what we would make in a year. We had no plan! "You need money? Take it out of the checking account." That was our plan.

Mom was amazing at staying on top of everything, but it wasn't the best way to handle our finances. At that time, we were totally unaware of GAAP—Generally Accepted Accounting Principles. We had no balance sheet. We were just adding and subtracting, doing everything based on cash. It was all in Mom's head! It truly is amazing how she did it, keeping everything straight, knowing exactly what she was doing. But it's no way to run a business.

We then hired Mike Redmond as our Chief Financial Officer. At the time, we were managing hundreds of millions of dollars using the spreadsheet program Excel. We had absolutely zero controls. Mike's first office was a janitor's closet— literally, a janitor's closet that we emptied and where we installed a desk. Initially, Mom and Dad were reluctant to show him the financials.

Eventually, we allowed Mike to start using QuickBooks. He preached to us over and over that we couldn't just be reactive—we needed to be able to forecast, to see where we were with specific markers and goals to get to where we wanted and needed to be. It took Mike three years to convince us we needed a plan.

Mike brought it up every quarter, but he kept getting resistance. Finally, after three years, he convinced us we needed a plan, and we started doing audits. Before that, we had no accountability and no controls. What a gift to us! Chris was able to convince this man who had a great job at a big company, Aetna, to join our family business, to use Excel, work out of a janitor's closet, and have no access to the financials at first. But Mike did it. He caught the vision, and he's still with us today.

Ron Williams, the former CEO of Aetna and the "CEO of CEOs" in healthcare, having turned the company around from barely breaking even to a Fortune 50 company and having trained a large number of the healthcare CEOs in America today, moved to Boca Raton, Florida. Ron is a graduate of MIT and extremely methodical. Chris reached out to Ron, who responded with tremendous generosity of his time and wisdom.

When Chris asked him at some point, "Why are you spending so much time with me, having dinner with me, investing in me?"

Ron said, "Because others invested in me."

Chris gives Ron credit for teaching him how to operate as a CEO. He learned what it means to transition from an inspirational, vision-based CEO to one who could actually execute and bring to fruition his inspired vision.

"Eighty percent of what I know about being a CEO, I learned from Ron Williams," Chris says. "The other 20 percent? Nineteen of that came from Horst Schulze of Ritz-Carlton and Jim Murray of Humana. These three men are three of the world's greatest operators of organizations. Only 1 percent of what I know about being a CEO came from books I read."

One of Chris's favorite quotes from Ron is, "It is not your job as CEO to give people the answers. It is your job as CEO to make sure they get to the right answers. Do not give them the answers."

Chris readily admits that's difficult for him—he's a problem-solver, and answers come to him very easily. To take that advice and run with it, we were forced to develop a system, a methodology, and a culture in which people drive to the right answer, without giving them those answers.

"I've learned to ask a lot of questions," Chris says. "Almost every time, the answer they come up with is better than the one I thought was right."

Reflecting on his learning and growth as the CEO of ChenMed, Chris says, "Every two years, I've had to reinvent myself in this position. The organization is growing so fast, it requires a different leadership mindset and methodology. I could not have done this by myself. Seven men have had a profound influence on me and have taught me how to be a CEO—Bob Kocher and Todd Johnson with McKinsey, Ron Williams, Bruce Broussard of Humana, Horst Schulze, Jim Murray, and my coach, Raymond Gleason. I would not be where I am, and ChenMed would not be where it is, without the guidance and support they have provided."

Gordon's journey was different. Developing a strong clinical leadership in which physicians drive culture, outcomes, and business performance is unique. There aren't many examples in the business world from which to learn. Further, the CMO role at ChenMed constantly evolved based on what we learned. We needed agility, problem-solving, mastery of the clinical talent life cycle, and building a strong culture for physicians that meshed well with other parts of the organization. ChenMed's strong culture of leadership development for physicians started and continues with Gordon at the helm.

Gordon's leadership journey is shaped heavily by raw experiential training and open and direct feedback from Chris, Mom, and Dad. But internal struggles and challenges along the way led to conflict and the need for external help. Gordon's first coach, Gregor Gardner, opened Gordon's eyes to a world of leadership tools and books, personality inventories, and self-awareness.

When considering the impact coaching had on him, Gordon remarks, "When I started with Gregor, I realized there were so many different leadership tools and frameworks. It was refreshing to dive into a world of personal growth and apply what I learned to my daily challenges. I was a dry sponge soaking up fresh water."

After Gregor, Gordon's next coach, Drew Lawson, focused on Gordon's "inner game." Drew had a profound impact on the development of his regular disciplines and routines, as well as intentional relationship development, starting with his most important relationships: God, Jessica, and his four children. "Drew's investment in my development has helped me grow in every aspect of my life and allowed me to develop a rhythm of growth, productivity, and prioritization," Gordon says.

Gordon's self-discovery spread to the rest of the family, as we learned how best to communicate and complement one another. Furthermore, Gregor's early coaching sessions inspired Gordon's continued thirst for more knowledge and wisdom— he dives into twenty to thirty books each year. Each has a focus on leadership and personal development. Patrick Lencioni and John C. Maxwell are two of his favorite authors. Despite all the reading, the essence of Gordon's leadership skills remains rooted in family. "Most of what I learned as a leader has come from guidance and feedback from Chris and my parents, with a big assist from my coaches," he says.

Just like when we were younger, Chris continues to invest in training Gordon, downloading all his learnings as he grows. As with many of the things we experience, we quickly share the experiences with our own team members. Because we've benefited from so much executive coaching and mentorship, we believe our physician and business leaders deserve the same investment. These leaders get poured into, with world-class executive coaching and top-notch leadership programs.

Gordon says, "Physicians all love to learn, grow, and lead, but few have the leadership training opportunity we offer at ChenMed. Further, fewer have the opportunity to gain leadership experience to master those skills. I love that we can give physicians the opportunity not only to grow into their fullest potential as leaders, but they can be a part of something much, much bigger than any of us can attain individually."

IN PREPARING to write this chapter, we talked extensively with Stephanie and Jessica about what it means to be a part of this family. Jessica used a phrase about us and our intentionality that resonated strongly in our dealings with one another: "We assume positive intent."

Think about the power of that statement. Even when we disagree strongly on any given subject, if we assume positive intent from the person with whom we strongly disagree, we are well on our way to being able to work things out. That phrase speaks to our trust, our love, and our belief in one another. We do have one another's best interests at heart, and we embrace one another's strengths and encourage one another as we pursue our opportunities.

Now we do that not only within our family but in our organization. It's countercultural in business. Today people assume negative intent, that others are out to get them, to take advantage of them. We operate differently. We're not out to get anybody—we're all going after the mission.

Mom and Dad started us on this journey the right way. Our job is to pass that on to our kids, so they can keep it going from generation to generation.

# CHAPTER 9

# HAPPY, HEALTHY, and HOME for the PANDEMIC

---

IN JANUARY 2020, we began to hear reports that COVID-19 had arrived in the United States. New York, especially, was heating up. By the end of January and into early February, we could see it was escalating. We started watching community spread and began getting concerned for our patients. Through February, we continued to monitor developments closely. We were hearing horrific reports of bodies piling up and hospital systems being overwhelmed.

Facilities were running out of ventilators, other necessary equipment, and personal protective equipment (PPE). Like nearly everyone else, not only those of us in the healthcare system, we were wondering: *What's going to happen? Will we become overwhelmed as well?*

As more and more data came available, we could see that

the virus was especially virulent for older patients, specifically those with chronic conditions and in minority populations. In other words, exactly the people we serve! Our patients were literally the ideal target for COVID. With that knowledge came an overwhelming sense of responsibility to take care of them.

We called an emergency meeting of the executive team.

"Guys, we are dealing with a threat that is perfectly designed to kill our patients," Chris said. "We take care of the old, the poor, and the sick. Exactly the population this virus is going after. What are we going to do about it?"

In those early days, we had no idea how the virus might impact younger people. Since the data pointed to seniors, we were concerned about our parents, but not ourselves.

"COVID doesn't go after us," we said at the time. "But we're responsible for our patients and need to make sure they're safe. There is no one else to protect our patients from this pandemic."

As February 2020 ended and March began, more statistics confirmed that the people who were dying were older. A preponderance of African Americans and Hispanics, diabetics, obese patients, and those with lung and heart disease were most at risk. Again, exactly the kind of conditions we commonly see in our patient population.

Jason Lane, Jessica's brother and Chris's roommate in college and med school, is an infectious disease specialist who works with us. Jason trained under Dr. Anthony Fauci.

We put Jason and Dr. Susan Schayes, who serves as our Chief Transformation Officer, in charge of leading our COVID response team. Jason led as the infectious disease expert for the company. Susan's skill as one of the key leaders at ChenMed is to anticipate needs while driving passion and energy to the efforts at hand. They met with our executive team to help craft our strategy.

Because of the technology and communication network Dad had developed across all our centers, we were able to institute hourly communication with one another. Our lines of rapid communication were like a military operation, using secure texts. Our response was even a few steps ahead of the federal government.

"We realized we had to be our own CDC," Gordon says. "We looked at the data, and to take care of our sickest patients, we started masking in our centers before anyone else. We screened for COVID before anyone else. We switched to virtual visits before anyone else. We were able to make that monumental pivot in seven days!"

Our Chief Information Officer, Hernando Celada, and our Associate Chief Medical Information Officer, Danny Guerra, oversaw the switch of our entire IT organization to virtual. Operations had to transform as well. Our Chief Operating Officer, Jason Barker, who runs our business operations, worked with Gordon and our clinical operations not only to protect our patients but also to protect our doctors and staff.

"Very early on, we made a commitment not to lose one staff member to COVID," Gordon says. Some of our doctors are seniors; we had to protect them. Because of our ages and good health, neither of us felt that we were at risk, but we were very protective of Mom and Dad. While we followed the CDC's safety precautions, we believed that if we did get COVID ourselves, it would be like getting a cold or the flu.

We told our older doctors and staff, "If you're over sixty, stay home and work remotely."

We had a couple of rallying cries. For our patients, we told them to stay *Healthy, Happy, and at Home!* For our staff, Dr. Susan Schayes came up with the slogan *Stay Calm and ChenMed On!* We made T-shirts with that phrase and gave them out to everyone.

Chris met with Mike Redmond, our CFO. "Mike, Ritz-Carlton has a no-questions-asked, open-the-checkbook policy if a customer has an issue. Anything under three hundred dollars, any employee can do whatever they need to do to solve a problem for a customer and make that guest happy. Can we open the checkbook for our employees to keep our patients healthy, happy, and at home?"

We went one step further and made the amount unlimited. If it was legal, anyone in our company could do whatever they needed to do to serve our patients during the pandemic. We got out the word: "Spend whatever you need so our patients stay healthy, happy, and at home."

Mike, who had spent the last eight years building controls on our spending and financials, found a way to make that happen. He and his team also tracked down the equipment needed to protect our team. We called the protective program for our people "Ludicrous Safety." Any protective equipment that Gordon, Dr. Jason Lane, Dr. Susan Schayes, or Jason

Barker said we needed, Mike and his team found and distributed it to every one of our centers.

Marke Dickinson, our Chief Marketing Officer, and Jim Whitling, our Chief Human Resources Officer, told us we needed to be in constant communication with our staff. Chris began a twice-weekly video presentation to inform, inspire, and commend our staff. Gordon and Jason created a series of meetings targeting different stakeholders. These meetings ran multiple times per week, and help from Drs. Lane and Schayes kept our organization on the same page. We were at war with COVID, and we had to train and equip our troops to survive and win the war. While Drs. Lane and Schayes bore the brunt of our outward-facing efforts, Stephen Greene, our Chief Administrative Officer, led the efforts from behind the scenes.

Three terms sum up how the people of ChenMed responded to the COVID attack on our patient population—*speed, intentionality,* and *love.* We didn't wait for someone to tell us what to do. We accessed the wealth of talent and wisdom among our staff and reacted quickly to COVID's threat. We weren't haphazard and chaotic in our response—we were intentional in applying our best resources to address the threat. And it all was motivated by love—love for our patients and love for one another. These three components produced beautiful results, keeping our people ludicrously safe and our patients healthy, happy, and at home.

Our technological connectivity proved critical in our ability to share what was working across all the centers. We even gave tablets to many of our patients so we could stay in constant contact with them. Our communication was instantaneous, and considering what the world around us was facing, our results were amazing. We focused on doing the right thing for our patients and empowered local leaders to adapt our corporate philosophy for their patient population.

We wrote out scripts for our centers to use in educating their patients on how best to deal with the pandemic. By enabling every center leader to do what was best for their community, we saw them accomplish beautiful things. In order to get the information out, ChenMed doctors were offering local town hall meetings. Many of them became the trusted voice in their communities, even as distrust in our government's response rose as everything became more and more politicized.

In one of our Zoom meetings, we heard from our center leader at the County Line Senior Center in Miami Gardens. They had begun weekly proactive check-ins by phone with every one of their patients. They called them "Love Calls."

"What a great idea!" we said. "Everyone should be doing this."

And in no time, they were. We didn't wait for a patient to ask for something; we anticipated their needs. "Whatever you think your patient needs, go get it for them," we said. "If they're too scared to go out, get them food, toilet paper, anything. Deliver it to their house. We will reimburse you for any and all expenses related to taking loving care of your patients."

Our lonely, anxious, scared, and depressed patients responded beautifully. On one of our calls, a doctor in Georgia told us, "I just got a Love Call back from one of my patients!"

We've heard many stories of our patients returning the love offered to them by praying for and thinking of us.

As of this writing, ChenMed has grown more in the last eighteen months than ever before. That growth took place because of the trust our physicians and staff built through their loving care of seniors by proactively reaching out to patients, especially during the pandemic. One of the great beauties of value-based care is that when you do the right thing for your patients, you get better results.

We ask one another, *What would you want done for your own family members?* Once we have an answer to that question, we say, *OK, go do that for our patients.*

# CHAPTER 10

# LIKE DYING
# in SOLITARY
# CONFINEMENT

---

*In the beginning of the book we said we were two voices telling the Chen story as one. In this chapter, we depart from that format. When Chris was hospitalized with COVID, it was a life-changing experience. He alone tells this story.*

AS OUR COMPANY, our nation, and our world responded to the spread of COVID, I was thinking—*I'm in great shape. I'm young and strong. I'll be fine. After all, I'm not in the demographic that has a problem with this. And even if I do get it, it will be mild, and then I'll be immune. Let's just get it over with.*

On June 22, 2020, our entire family, all fourteen of us (Mom and Dad, Gordon, Jessica, and their four kids, and Stephanie and me with our four), were getting ready to leave on a trip to Colorado. Before leaving, and although none of us had any symptoms, we did the responsible thing and went in for a COVID test. Surprisingly, though she was asymptomatic, Stephanie's test came back positive.

"I did have a bit of a headache, and I felt tired that day," Stephanie said. "But Chris told me, 'Stephanie, you're a mom. With four kids. And you have a full-time, very demanding job. You're always tired with a headache!'"

Meanwhile, that very morning, I went into work and was bragging to my assistant about what great shape I was in. I'd had knee surgery about a year before, but I had worked my way back into triathlon-competing race condition. The pandemic had served to spur me on to take my training to the next level. My swimming, biking, and running speeds were right where I wanted them to be for a race.

But just like the Good Book says, "Haughtiness goes before the fall" (Proverbs 16:18).

That night, my temperature climbed to one hundred three degrees. For the next four or five days, I ran a fever and felt much worse than I ever had with a case of the flu. After that fourth or fifth day, however, I felt much better. Then I thought, *Thank goodness it's over. Going through that wasn't worth the immunity, but as they say, what doesn't kill you makes you stronger. Now I'm good to go.*

When am I going to learn? That very night, my fever came back with a vengeance in a second phase of COVID. It was even worse than before.

After three more days of running a fever well over a hundred, Stephanie asked, "Chris, how many days can you have a fever like this?"

"Not too many," was about all I could muster.

When I got out of bed to take a shower, I felt really dizzy. I called Jason, Jessica's brother, who along with Dr. Susan Schayes was running lead on our COVID response team.

"Jason, I really don't feel right. In fact, I feel sick as a dog."

After I described exactly what I was feeling and how long I had been running a fever, Jason said, "Chris, you need to go get this checked out. Go to the emergency room, now."

I've been around hospitals and have seen what happens in them for most of my life. Before leaving the house, I sat down separately with both of my sons. It wasn't because I thought something awful would happen, but because, well, you just never know. I wanted them to be prepared. First I talked with the oldest, James, who was sixteen at the time.

"James, listen," I said. "Daddy's going to the hospital right now. If for any reason, Daddy doesn't come back, you are the man of the house. You need to act like it. Everything that you need to know is in the Chen family mission. I've trained you to live your life by the standards of that mission. If there's anything else you need, you will find it in the Bible and your faith in Christ."

James was a bit traumatized by what I said. I then called in John, who was thirteen, and basically said the same thing to him. His response was similar to his older brother's. To Stephanie and the girls, all I told them was that I was doing what Jason suggested—I was going to get myself checked out.

BECAUSE OF OUR STRONG relationship with our local hospital,

I was able to go in the back door. I was so weak, someone had to bring out a wheelchair and wheel me into a private room. I didn't have to wait long for them to check my oxygen levels. I know how to read those things and was happy to see my numbers were not too bad.

"Chris, I want to get a CAT scan," the emergency room doctor said.

"Why?" I asked. Here I was, thinking I would be going back home soon.

"Well, you're breathing really fast. Twenty-two times a minute."

I guess it was because of all my endurance training that I hadn't realized how much of a struggle it was to breathe. I hadn't even noticed it. I'm used to sucking it up and enduring any discomfort when I work out. I tried to argue with him. Finally he got through to me with this: "Chris, you need to be a patient."

Doctors are notorious for being the worst patients. We call one another out, when necessary, with those words.

"Fine," I said, "if you're going to use that gun against me."

They ran the CAT scan and everybody freaked out. You could see that I had pneumonia in all five lobes of my lungs. Being in race shape probably saved my life, but it had also masked the severe state I was in.

I was admitted into the intensive care unit, and they loaded me up on every therapy they could find. The problem was that two of the key therapies they wanted to use—plasma and Remdesivir—weren't available.

I sent the pictures of my lungs from the CAT scan to Ivan Castellon, a close friend I went to medical school with who's a radiologist at Jackson Memorial and the University of Miami medical school. I wanted to get his read on my condition.

"Well, if it makes you feel any better," he said in his dry, straightforward way, "it's not the worst case I've seen."

"Thanks, man," I said and hung up. This was concerning. It was a big blow. I finally realized that I was only a few quick, shallow breaths away from going on a ventilator. My medical degree and business experience and all my swimming, cycling, and CrossFit workouts couldn't help me. I wondered what life would be like for my wife, my children, my parents, my patients, and my work family without me.

BEFORE THIS HAPPENED, I was naïve about life on the other side of the ICU glass. One of my strongest skills coming out of medical training was critical care. I conducted countless blood gas procedures but had never had one done to me. I was immune to the constant din of hospital bells and alarms, but I had never heard them from a hospital bed. I never knew the feeling of being strapped down and poked and prodded every few hours for blood draws and injections. While I knew the jumble of cords and wires coming out of my patients made it hard for them to move, I now feel foolish suggesting that they "try to get some sleep."

I knew how to treat ICU patients but I had no idea what it was like to be an ICU patient. And when you're an ICU patient with COVID, it is like dying in solitary confinement.

The hospital was fantastic. I knew many of the doctors, including the Chief Medical Officer, Fabio, and the Chief of Cardiology, Roberto. They would walk by the window and knock on the glass. Then they would call my cell phone and reassure me that I was in good hands.

Still, a feeling of despondency overcame me. Then the questions began: *Am I going to be a statistic? Will Stephanie no longer have a husband? Will our children be fatherless? Who will take care of them? Are they ready for this?* I imagined not having a funeral and what that would do to my parents. My life as a CEO felt far away, but when I did think about ChenMed, I remembered our fantastic leadership team. I knew the company was in good hands.

So there I was, facing the possibility of my impending death. My focus centered in on what was truly important to me—my relationships with my wife, my children, my family. Deep sadness overwhelmed me as I thought about not being able to let Stephanie know how much I love her, to hug and invest in my children. That was all I cared about as I laid in that hospital bed.

OVER THE NEXT thirty-six hours, my condition showed no improvement. I felt like I was staring into a dark tunnel—standing alone on the train tracks without my family, or any human contact, for that matter. Sure, the doctors would review my numbers and call on the phone to speak with me. Nurses would come in frequently but fully gowned and only for two minutes or less. I was alone and I was lonely.

The nights were the worst. That's when the fevers were the highest and my breathing the most labored. I felt like I was wasting away: covered in sweat, unable to bathe or shower, tied down by cords, and trying to breathe. *Is this how my heart failure patients feel when they cannot breathe and are drowning from the inside out?* I wondered.

One bright spot during those dark days was my friend Bob Kocher. He's the man who helped me through Dad's illness, and he was there for me during my own. Bob would call, ever the Energizer Bunny—upbeat, cracking jokes, trying to keep me entertained and my mind off my deteriorating condition. We would hang up, however, and the machines and their numbers didn't lie. I was back to being alone, facing reality.

Wednesday, my third day in the hospital, was the hardest day. I felt like the ICU bed was swallowing me and taking me further away from everything I knew. I prayed for hope. But I was getting worse, and I was still only number three on the waiting list for Remdesivir and convalescent plasma (spun down blood from someone who had recovered from COVID), which is filled with antibodies against the virus.

Lying there, I recalled an episode from when I was first becoming a doctor. Because of my training in cardiology, I spent lots of time in critical care units, working with the sickest patients suffering from coronary disease. One night, there was a lady in the waiting room, wailing. Her husband had died in the emergency room.

"Oh, my God, oh, my God. Is this how it happens? Is

this how it happens?" She said it over and over. "We were just having dinner!" she said.

I found out that her husband had stage four cancer. I thought, *How can you be surprised? How could you not realize that this was a possibility?*

I then remembered the day Dad had the seizure and almost died. We had been watching football together. He looked like a normal person. We all knew he was sick, but he seemed to be doing so well. In fact, he was doing so well that Stephanie and I left him with Mom, Gordon, and Jessica, sitting there in front of the TV, and went out for a dinner date.

Later, in the emergency room that night, when I was dealing with Dad's brain bleed and his blood thinners, what that woman meant and experienced hit me—*He was just right here! He seemed to be doing fine!*

Now, years after Dad's experience, I was the one lying there, and the thought kept going through my mind, over and over, just like that woman said—*Is this the way it happens?*

Systematically, God took everything away from me. I realized, *I have nothing. My strong, great body, normally in shape—gone. In this condition, I can't lead our company. I can't be a father to my children. I can't be a husband to my wife.* I felt totally helpless and totally useless.

I was wasting away. I hadn't showered in four days. I couldn't go to the bathroom. I couldn't even walk. In a matter of days I had gone from having everything—an amazing wife, great kids, incredible resources, a beautiful purpose and vision, the ability to lead with dignity something that was life-changing for thousands and thousands of people—to nothing. And this had all happened in just one horrific week.

I felt sad and hopeless. Psychologically, I was dying, alone. I was watching my numbers go in the wrong direction, and I knew very clearly what they meant, the story they were telling. Sometimes it's better not to know.

THAT NIGHT, Helen showed up for her night shift. Helen is a six-foot-tall Jamaican ICU nurse, but I'm pretty sure she was a marine drill instructor in another life. She started by changing my gown and sheets. She helped me take a chlorhexidine towel bath. Helen is no-nonsense. If she wanted me to sit on the edge of the bed and I said "No," we reached an understanding. I sat on the edge of the bed.

Sometimes I fell asleep, but every hour or so Helen would open the door and yell, "Chris, c'mon, you've got to breathe. Breathe for me."

I knew what she was doing. I would take a few faster breaths and then the alarm would stop. If I didn't continue to breathe on my own, I was going on a ventilator. And from that point, I knew my mortality rate increased dramatically. I really believe Helen kept me alive that night.

Around 3:00 a.m. Helen came in again. When I heard her voice, I was already well-trained. As I took my faster breaths, Helen said, "Chris, your plasma has arrived. I'm going to get it."

What? The plasma wasn't supposed to get there for a couple of days.

"Are you sure?" I asked.

She replied, "The blood bank just called."

All I could say was, "Praise God." This was my first glimmer of hope.

I received the plasma as the shift changed in the morning.

"Thank you, Helen, for getting me through last night," I said as she left.

THE FOLLOWING MORNING, Gordon called. He had been in the background, working tirelessly, serving as my PCP. As nice and caring as each individual caregiver at the hospital had been, it really was a mess. Chaotic. Uncoordinated. The pulmonologist never spoke with the infectious disease doctor. In that system, the left hand doesn't know what the right hand is doing. There had been no single point person, a person of accountability, looking out for me.

But just as I had been that person when we found out about Dad's cancer, and every PCP at ChenMed now serves as that person for their patients, Gordon was crusading for me—talking to specialists, trying to figure out what should be done. Gordon was calling everyone, chasing it down, pursuing every possibility he could think of to try and get Remdesivir for me. When he called that morning, he said they had secured the drug and I would get my first dose at 11:00 a.m.

I found out later that Gordon had convinced them to split doses of Remdesivir. They gave me someone else's day five. When mine came in, someone else got my end doses.

After close to ten days of fevers, my temperature returned

to normal. My breathing stabilized. That afternoon, I began to feel better. I was moved to a chair. I wondered, *Are the plasma and Remdesivir working?* I was afraid to get my hopes up again. I'd thought the worst of it was over once before, but that had only been the calm before the storm.

Thursday became Friday and I remained fever-free. I got a good night's sleep on Friday night, and when Saturday morning rolled around, I felt completely different. My lung volumes were up, and I could walk around my room without losing my breath. I was ready to go home. I called Stephanie.

"I need to come home," I said. "I'm ready."

She told Mom and Dad that I had called.

"Do not let him come home. He's too sick!" Mom said.

"No. He's much better, Mommi," Stephanie insisted. "He says he needs to come home. I believe him. I'm going to get him."

As Yvonne, the nurse, wheeled me out of my ICU room, I looked around. The hall was reserved for COVID patients. When I arrived, more than half the rooms were empty. That day, the rooms were full and many of the occupants were on ventilators. I knew the statistics—only half of those who require ventilators ever leave the hospital. I asked Yvonne to stop so I could pray for my fellow COVID brothers and sisters. Then Yvonne wheeled me downstairs.

Stephanie and James were waiting. Ask anybody who knows me—I am not an emotional person. But in that moment, I was overcome. We hugged and cried, holding one another tightly. For the first time since entering the ICU, I realized I would still be a husband, father, brother, son, and once again lead ChenMed. The realization that God would allow me to continue in these roles overwhelmed me. It was the greatest blessing ever.

Not long after I got out of the hospital, I found out that ChenMed had made *Fortune* magazine's Change the World list. It's a huge honor and a great boost for our company. Then I started getting calls about a medical group that had copied our model, led by a person who considered himself a "competitor." He was a man whose ways I took issue with. His company was smaller than ChenMed, and they weren't getting anything close to the results we have with our patients. While I was recovering, his company went public, valued at $15 billion.

One person said on the phone, "Now I can appreciate what you've built at ChenMed even more, because you're a much better and much larger version of what that guy has built!"

Who would have thought that he would be creating this kind of relevancy for our company? I thought, *I can't be mad at that guy anymore!*

All these wonderful things for our company happened while I wasn't working. And isn't that just how God works?

My recovery was extremely slow. Each day, I thought, *Could I live like this? Only able to walk five steps?* If I can be with my wife and my kids, I thought, *Yes!* I knew I could live like that. The next day, I took twenty steps. And I knew I could live like that.

As strange as it may sound, this was perhaps the best thing that ever happened to me. To have everything taken away from me, stripped down to nothing in a week's time, and then, over a period of three months, gradually getting one thing back each day. I came to appreciate each one of my many blessings as the gifts they are and how valuable and precious they are to me.

I was not allowed to come back to work for six weeks. My family cut me off, taking away my phone. I had no access to anything for that entire time. My family was traumatized, and we had difficulty talking about it. We went to counseling to help us get past it. Stephanie felt guilty, believing she was the person who had given it to me. She needed healing from that. I still have some weird pains occasionally, even though I am back to my training again.

Once I was allowed to return to work, it didn't take long for me to realize that I still needed to take it slowly. Prior to getting COVID myself, I had hosted a half-hour-long Zoom meeting every month for our leaders and partners. My first or second week back, I decided to host one. After about five minutes into it, my strength was gone. I had to get off and let one of the other executives carry the remaining twenty-five minutes.

As my slow recovery continued, one day I said to Stephanie, "You know, I haven't had a cheeseburger in three or four years. I think I want one." My body was probably craving protein to rebuild itself. I got about halfway done and had to choke down the rest. But I wasn't about to give up.

Prior to this experience, I thought I knew a lot about COVID. I was wrong. Now I have a perspective that I wouldn't wish on anyone. Still, the questions keep coming: *How many people in this country don't have access to the acute care I received? How many more can't call upon a company of prayer warriors and a family of doctors to look after them? What do these people do? And how does God want me to use what I've learned moving forward?*

I am still searching for answers to these questions.

# CHAPTER 11

# LOVE, ACCOUNTABILITY, and PASSION

THE TWO OF US are who we are because of our parents'
values. They didn't just teach us how to live and how to treat
others with their words; they have modeled it for us every day
of our lives in the way they live theirs. As our children grew,
we realized we needed to put a family mission statement into
words that could be passed on from generation to generation.
What we arrived at, in seven simple statements, came from
unpacking what God had already put in our hearts and then
clarifying it with the right language—what we want future
generations to know and embrace about what it means to be a
member of the Chen family.

All six adults—Dad and Mom, Chris and Stephanie,
Gordon and Jessica—participated in the process. During six
half-day meetings over a six-month period, we were guided by

Skip Perkins and Mike Jeffries, two men who help lead our Chen family office. Everyone contributed, bringing in our favorite Bible verses and how we as a family live out what these Scriptures express. As the two extreme extroverts in the group, the two of us probably did most of the talking. But everyone got to have their input to and approval of the final language.

Here's what we came up with for the Chen Family Mission Statement:

1.  Know, love, and serve the one, true Triune God.

2.  Love one another, starting with family.

3.  Appreciate God's blessing of living, working, and being together as a family.

4.  Work hard and persevere.

5.  Seek wisdom, education, and lifelong learning.

6.  Promote health.

7.  Pass these values down to and invest in future generations.

We recognize that there are cultural components that shape who we are—the emphasis on work, and honoring wisdom and generations that have gone before, for example. Those may seem very un-American today, but as Dad and Mom have reminded us, we're drawing on five thousand years of history with a multigenerational approach. Add to that the Judeo-Christian tradition informed by the Bible's thousands of years of wisdom, and we understand why it's important to set things up that will impact and inform multiple generations.

Just as Mom expected of us as kids, we pass along to our children the highest of expectations, within their God-given unique gifts and abilities. As she says, "Inspect what you expect." We tell them to aim high. And we provide accountability on their progress. From Dad, we learned to do that with patience and kindness. Full love *and* full accountability—these two extremes, as modeled for us by our parents, are what we are passing along to future Chen generations.

One of the many things we love about these seven values is that we can keep them fresh and alive by having each day of the week correspond to one of the seven points. This works right down the line, from Sunday through Saturday. On Sunday, we start the week with a focus on God. So number one, "Know, love, and serve the one, true Triune God," is a natural to correspond with every Sunday. And the mission statement ends with number seven, "Pass these values down to and invest in future generations," on Saturday, which is the day we normally devote to rest as our Sabbath and intentionally spend time with our kids. These seven reminders provide a flow and rhythm of life that give focus to every day, making them beautiful daily themes with a weekly cadence.

As mentioned earlier, and to reinforce these with our children, we've instituted what has come to be called a "Chen mitzvah." When they reach age twelve, we have a coming-of-age ceremony for each child. The budding Chen adult recites the Chen Family Mission Statement from memory in front of the whole family. That's followed by a big celebration of love and wisdom that gets poured into that child. Each family member writes them a personal letter and offers gifts. We began performing this ceremony around 2016.

Our children have responded very positively to this tradition. The mission statement's seven points are simple but deep with meaning, serving as guideposts for life. Our kids embrace their initiation into the Chen family as a young adult and appreciate no longer being considered a kid. We are intentional in doing this differently than most Americans in our culture today. Once they've had their Chen mitzvah, our children are held to a higher standard as a young adult. They continue to receive training from the other adults but are now in the process of maturing until the age of twenty, when they are expected to be and act as an adult. Not out on their own, but now as a participating adult member of our united Chen family.

ONCE WE HAD done this work for our family, and as ChenMed continued to grow, we realized we needed something similar for the way we serve our patients. We articulated the ChenMed Vision—*To be America's leading primary care provider, transforming care of the neediest populations.*

The vision alone wasn't enough. We saw that we needed to articulate how to achieve the vision, which led us to the ChenMed Mission: *We honor seniors with affordable VIP care that delivers better health.*

Even with a clearly stated vision to achieve and a mission to deliver, we recognized a need for guideposts—like with our family statement—to direct us and help us assess how well we were implementing them. That led to establishing the ChenMed Values and Behaviors.

### ChenMed Values and Behaviors

With input from our executive team and several external consultants, we narrowed our values down to three—Love, Accountability, and Passion. To help measure how we were living out those values, we came up with four or five behaviors for each one. Here's the language we use to communicate our values and behaviors to every ChenMed employee:

## LOVE

L1. Serve others with empathy and selflessness. Ensure that personal wants are secondary.

L2. Treat patients, their families/caregivers, and colleagues with respect, kindness, and dignity as they are a beautiful creation of God.

L3. Openly invest in others to help them grow and develop.

L4. Actively provide feedback to fellow employees with courage to constructively support each person to achieve our company vision and mission.

## ACCOUNTABILITY

A1. Take ownership of commitments and follow through to achieve excellent results.

A2. Inspect what you expect.

A3. Own the problem, see it to resolution, and don't make or accept excuses.

A4. Humbly acknowledge weaknesses, mistakes, and improvement opportunities that enable personal and company growth.

A5. Build trust as someone who can be counted on by others to consistently deliver expectations.

## PASSION

P1. Aim high and work with a sense of urgency to achieve our stated company goals.

P2. Pursue our mission every day with renewed dedication; never get complacent.

P3. Consistently bring inspiring energy that encourages others to do more and do better.

P4. Relentlessly identify ways to immediately improve, and work toward achieving sustainable results by investing in people and processes.


WE DID GET SOME pushback on using "Love" and its corresponding behaviors as one of our ChenMed values. When Chris ran them by his CEO coach, Raymond Gleason with Building Champions, Raymond told Chris it wasn't a good idea. "Don't do this," he said. "Don't use the word *love*; it's not corporate enough. Too *frou-frou.*"

Raymond also didn't think that the second behavior under Love should include the phrase "a beautiful creation of God." He felt like it would be imposing our religious opinions on our employees.

The second pushback came from Marke Dickinson, our Chief Marketing Officer, and Jim Whitling, our Chief Human Resources Officer. While they both share our faith, they had the same response as Raymond to the use of this language in our corporate values and behaviors. For Chris, rather than convincing him not to go forward, it did the opposite.

"Guys, I was on the fence as to whether to do this," Chris told them. "There are seminal moments in our lives, key decision-making situations that will be played back for us when we stand before God's judgment seat. This is one of those moments. If I had been left to my own devices, I may well have chickened out and not used this language. But now that you've challenged me on it, I know we have to do it."

Thinking back on that pivotal moment, Chris has further thoughts. "I'm not sure if God was testing me or not. But I knew it was a defining moment. We could not sweep who we are under the rug and hide behind typical corporate, bureaucratic language. The combination of those three men, who have my best interests—and ChenMed's best interests—at heart was compelling. They were so respectful and kind in the way they shared their concerns. But I knew in the core of my being that we had to go against them."

How often have you heard of corporations, or even

individuals, that articulate their vision or mission or something similar to our values and behaviors, and then it doesn't go any further than a sign hung on the wall or a piece of paper gathering dust in a file cabinet? To protect against that, we've instituted several ways to keep ours fresh, alive, and put into practice every day.

For example, team leaders start their meetings with "the ChenMed Way," a slide that reviews our vision, mission, core model, and values. Chris learned this technique from Ron Williams and Horst Schulze, who come from two very different industries.

"I don't usually act immediately on advice I get from one person," Chris says. "I'll say, 'That is very interesting. I will think about how we might be able to incorporate that at ChenMed.' But when I get the same thing from two powerhouses such as Ron and Horst, I know it's time to put it into practice. We're going to execute it, and we're going to do it beautifully."

The purpose is to remind everyone of what we are committing to and further provide opportunities to reflect on our "why." We identify how our values and behaviors are being implemented. Various team members remind each other of key values and behaviors they want to celebrate by sharing examples of how they have seen others exhibit the behaviors in the past week. They may also share something personal, especially under Accountability, to acknowledge any area in their own practice that needs improvement.

In one meeting with his team, Gordon pointed to himself as he read A4—"Humbly acknowledge weaknesses, mistakes, and improvement opportunities that enable personal and company growth." He identified four "crutches" he had been leaning on as a leader, which, once identified, he could address and be held accountable to his team to correct. In that same meeting, several other leaders identified their team members who exhibited P1 under the Passion value—"Aim high and work with a sense of urgency to achieve our stated company goals." They acknowledged and praised specific behaviors, performed excellently and with passion by members of their teams.

Here are just a few of these behaviors: Following a devastating hurricane that hit one of our markets, Vijay Jaligam, one of our CMOs, went to the homes of patients with no electricity to check on them and remind them that we were still available to meet their health needs. Our Market Clinical Manager for the region had a working ice maker and brought ice to insulin-dependent patients to keep their insulin cold. Team members from surrounding regions drove upwards of twelve hours with food and supplies to help the community, starting with our patients in the worst-hit areas. Our culture team and other home office team members flew in to bring more support and identified employees who needed financial assistance through our ChenMed Cares program, a nonprofit in which employees can donate to support other employees in times of need. All donations to ChenMed Care are matched by the Chen Family Foundation.

Here are a few more stories of the people of ChenMed acting upon Love, Accountability, and Passion:

Abigail Ramos, a Care Promoter at East Orlando, noticed a patient was sitting in a car that had broken down in the center's back parking lot. After speaking with him, she learned he was living in his car and trying to get to his family but he'd run out of gas. On her lunch break, Abigail went home to grab a gas can, filled it with gas, and came back to fill up the gentleman's tank.

Carmen Hernandez, a Care Promoter at the East Orlando Center, had a patient who was beginning to experience COVID symptoms after her daughter tested positive for COVID. The patient needed to be tested but was unable to get to the center because she has dementia, and her daughter was too sick to drive her. Carmen took it upon herself to obtain the proper PPE, a COVID test, and go to the patient's home to test her.

Tony Nguyen, a Member Growth Consultant (MGC) in New Orleans received a call from a patient he rescued who needed his roof repaired quickly because of bad weather. The patient didn't have anyone to call or help him, so he called Tony. After working a full day at the center, Tony went home to feed his dog, changed clothes, and headed over to the patient's home to assist with repairing his roof.

Bill Livingston, an MGC for Largo Center, has helped several patients either find housing or find subsidized alternatives. Recently he helped two patients find an apartment through a local partnership. He also rented a moving van for them, using his own funds, and helped load their belongings into it.

Neishma Rivera Mejias, Front Desk Team Lead in

Jacksonville, developed a personal bond with one of the patients. The patient had an upcoming appointment with a specialist but was going to miss it due to transportation delays. Neishma knew how important it was for the patient to go to this appointment and requested permission to take the patient to the appointment herself. The patient's appointment would have been delayed another six weeks had she not transported him.

Semaj Franklin and Holli Webb, MGCs from Metairie, LA, assisted a distressed patient with a flat tire. After they removed the flat tire and replaced it with the spare, they took the patient to the tire store to get a new standard-sized tire put on her vehicle. They waited with her until the process was completed and they were confident she could be on her way safely.

At another of our centers, one of our older male patients had his ex-wife move back in with him. It was a very unhealthy and unsafe environment for him—she was an illegal drug user, and she had her drug-using friends in and out of the house. Our patient was being taken advantage of by her and her friends. One of our case managers saw what was going on and stepped in to help.

First, she found state-funded housing for the patient to get him away from the unsafe situation. But he had no way to furnish it. That's when the care promoter stepped up.

"I have furniture he can have," she said. "But I don't have a way to get it to him." She's a small, slight woman who wouldn't have the strength to lift a couch or a bed, and she didn't have a vehicle to transport them in either.

That's when a driver from another center in that same city

heard about it and said he would take care of it. Using his own money, he rented a van, got a strong friend to help, picked up the furniture from the care promoter's home, and delivered it to the patient's new home. That's how the people of ChenMed put our values and behaviors into practice.

Think how easy it would be for an employee who gets paid by the hour to rationalize why it wasn't up to them to take action like the ones we've just described.

"It's not my job."

"I don't know that person."

"I don't have the time, money, strength, and so on."

But at every level of our organization, we have stories of Love, Accountability, and Passion in executing them. These actions weren't taken reluctantly or just to get an "attaboy" or "attagirl." In every one of those stories, our folks were excited and thrilled to be able to put the ChenMed Way into practice and make our patients healthier. Going above and beyond their job descriptions is common among the people of ChenMed. It's never the minimum—our folks figure out how to help our patients when they have a need. Any need.

We do give everyone the opportunity to provide us with feedback on our values and behaviors through our annual Speak-up Surveys and quarterly Pulse Surveys. These anonymous surveys are dedicated to reinforcing and measuring how we are doing with keeping our values front and center. Values and behaviors are used in quarterly employee reviews, which are built into annual reviews. This elevates them in importance and helps to keep them on the minds and in the hearts of everyone at ChenMed.

Our values and behaviors have also led to us to make some very tough decisions—letting employees go who weren't living up to the values. If someone is too focused on their own image and advancement while putting others down or if they take advantage of the organization while putting their personal agendas ahead of our vision and mission, they don't last with us. As you might imagine, Mom doesn't tolerate people she believes are toxic to the organization.

"Let them go," she says. But she then gives a generous severance when she does to make sure they land on their feet.

As Chris moved into the position of CEO of ChenMed, he hired Raymond Gleason as his business coach. Raymond taught Chris the difference between conditional and unconditional relationships.

"Chris," he said, "you are a family of faith. But you're not running a religious organization! You're running a business, and that business must achieve a goal. The goal is more important than any one individual. Every individual in that business must serve reaching the goal. The business exists to reach a certain goal and serve its purpose, so every person in the organization has a conditional role in the business. You can love them, take care of them, treat every person with honor and kindness, dignity, and joy. But at the end of the day, people at ChenMed are in the organization to achieve that common purpose and deliver ChenMed's vision and mission—to be America's leading primary care provider, to transform care of the neediest populations, and to honor seniors with affordable VIP care that delivers better health. Therefore, if an employee cannot meet their conditional responsibilities and requirements, as the leader, Chris, you must replace that person with someone who can."

Thinking back on that, Chris says, "Folks from our faith tradition often don't get this. We struggle with it. But Raymond is so right. We hire a person conditionally to achieve something that helps the company fulfill its purpose and meet its goals. As people of faith, how we do that matters. But it doesn't change the purpose of the business."

Our vision is to transform care for the neediest populations. The word *transform* is a result. Our mission is to deliver better health. That, too, is a result. We can measure that with numbers—reduced hospitalization rates, for example. We don't say, "I'm going to try." No. ChenMed exists to *achieve* that result. Employees must know they are conditionally employed to help ChenMed accomplish those results. And we tell that story with numbers.

Raymond didn't let Chris off in that discussion by only talking about other employees. He spoke to Chris about his role as CEO and a member of the Chen family too. "Chris, you don't have the right to allow the company to not achieve its purpose and goals because you aren't doing your job as the leader. And I get it. It's tricky. You are working with your family, and family is made up of unconditional relationships. But you must understand that in working with your family, you are all in *unconditional* relationships doing *conditional* jobs."

The good news for us is that all the members of our family are insanely committed to performance and their responsibility to serve the purpose and goals of ChenMed. Even so, it is a challenge at times. We have to remind ourselves periodically of that distinction between unconditional family relationships and conditional business relationships.

This eventually led Chris to go to Dad and tell him that we needed a board for ChenMed. Dad said, "Why, Chris, do we need a board? We're doing so well. That's expensive. Why?"

"Dad, number one: I need a boss," Chris said. "I have a job to do as the CEO of ChenMed. And I need oversight and accountability. I need you to be the chairman of the board—as my boss—with a group of people who report to you—on your board—to tell me the kind of job I'm doing as CEO of ChenMed. Because I have a conditional job, you need a place where you can comfortably lead and make sure that I am doing a good job in that role. When I'm not doing a good job, someone needs to put their big finger in my face and tell me what I'm doing wrong and make me fix it. We also need to bring outside people in, people who can say if we are doing a good job. We need their wisdom and perspective."

Dad agreed. "It's the order of the universe!" Chris says. "Honor your father and your mother. That order was not being maintained with me as CEO and Dad in a position in which he was below me in the business."

Now Chris presents possibilities to Dad that come from outside ChenMed, and Dad makes the final decision. Chris spoke with leaders of a number of successful companies—Ritz-Carlton, Chick-fil-A, Healthspring, Walgreens, Walmart, Amazon, and Tesla, to name a few. People who have solved many issues both in other industries and in healthcare. Today we have seven members of our board—Dad, Mom, Chris, Gordon, and three external members who cycle through for three-year terms.

In 2018, ChenMed didn't meet expectations. At a meeting of the board, Chris gave that announcement and was then moved on to the next topic. Horst Schulze stopped him. "Before we continue, Chris, we need to bathe in our failure," he said. "These results are because of these reasons"—which he enumerated—"and you"—pointing at Chris—"made this call. Let's be clear."

Chris remembers how everyone in the room went silent. Finally, he spoke.

"You're right," Chris said. "I made this call, and it was a big mistake. And here's what we're going to do to fix it."

Dad sat there and enjoyed it. He was very happy to have a board going forward.

Ever since that time, whenever we acknowledge a mistake or a failure, we articulate how we're going to fix it. Immediately after that, we exceed our goals and expectations. Every single time.

IN CORPORATE AMERICA in publicly traded companies, people are always watching their backs. Things typically move very slowly, with lots of bureaucracy, misalignment, missing purpose, and lack of trust. It's very rare when these elements aren't present. But we have none of those in our family, and we don't allow them to infiltrate ChenMed. In fact, we have the opposite.

We are transparent, make decisions at blistering speed, have tons of constructive conflict, and are unapologetic in our commitment to our vision, mission, and values. We've brought in outside people to survey our employees multiple times. What they have discovered is that we have ninety-five percent engagement with the mission of the company. The outsiders tell us they've never seen this level of commitment in an organization our size.

The reason—there's no red tape and bureaucracy, and there are no back channels to manipulate personal agendas. If these ever start to develop, we root them out and those people who started them aren't with the company for very long. We go direct. We give feedback to everyone, including ourselves. And we openly talk about weaknesses. That level of openness isn't for everyone. There is no place to hide at ChenMed. If you don't deliver results, we are going to talk about it. Everything is brought out in the open.

We let people know that if you are a person who gets locked up, who can't make a decision, you will get left behind; ChenMed is not a place for you. Moving as fast as we do, sometimes we break things. Of course, we don't try to break things, but it happens because we're willing to take risks to do the right thing rather than sit still because we're afraid of doing the wrong thing. There are only two areas where we refuse to take a risk. One—with the health of our patients. We will never put a patient's health and safety at risk. And two—with compliance of health standards and the law. Those two things are nonnegotiable. But with everything else, everyone at ChenMed is encouraged to take risks to do the right thing when it comes to achieving our vision and delivering our mission.

Chris told his team, "You only have to do two things to be a part of my team. Just two. One—you have to build your own great team. Find people at a high level of talent. They should be as talented as you are in their level of expertise so they can fully complement you and provide what your team needs. And they must work well as a team—know what it means not to look out for their own self-interests but to always have the team's best interests in mind. Two—you must make hard decisions. Do you have the right people doing the jobs you need done with excellence? If not, you have a hard decision to make. And you must effectively negotiate strategic trade-offs. We can't do everything. So what are the most important things? If a decision means sacrificing something, can you recognize the less crucial element to sacrifice so that greater good results from your decision? That's it. Build a great team yourself and make the hard decisions. That's all I ask of members of my team."

In speaking to his team and the executive council (the top fifty executives of ChenMed), he said, "At this level, I trust your character and I trust your work ethic. You will not get fired for making mistakes. But you will get fired for not recognizing, owning, and learning from your mistakes quickly enough."

Bureaucracies say, "Cover yourself, cover yourself, cover yourself." Give yourself "plausible deniability." We say, "Do not cover yourself. Go boldly and do what you think is best if it serves the mission, the vision, the purpose, and goals of ChenMed. You're going to make mistakes. And it's OK. *You will not get fired for making mistakes.*"

Often it can become a question of ego. We tell one another, "Don't stick to your guns if the numbers don't support the story you're telling or if you have no story to back up the numbers you're giving us. Own it, recognize it, learn from it—in fact, we value you MORE when you do that! Because when you do, you're getting closer to the real answer."

On our family trip to Atlanta, we met with key leaders who run Chick-fil-A. Out of that relationship, we learned another important lesson we could apply to ChenMed—the importance of localization. We give autonomy to those leading our centers, the men and women who know the culture and specific needs of their communities. We empower and encourage local markets to express themselves with tremendous ownership and autonomy while executing our standardized model.

WHEN WE LIVE our values and behaviors, we transform healthcare for our seniors. Having learned these key concepts from the Bible, we know the enduring impact these values can have along with the importance of holding to our values through good times and bad. How we treat others reflects what is in our hearts, and living our values allows us to spread God's love and healing. By holding one another to these values, our impact will transcend multiple generations and perhaps even millennia. *This* is what transforms hearts and transforms communities. Having the right values and behaviors is what allows us to build something that has deep and enduring impact. The most important component of whether we will succeed at scaling the ChenMed model to communities across America will be our ability to consistently build a strong culture through living our values rather than merely talking about them.

# CHAPTER 12

# A CITY
# on a HILL

IN THE GREATEST speech ever given, a small-town carpenter in the Middle East compared the light required to overcome darkness to placing a city on a hill. In that famous speech two thousand years ago, Jesus said that you don't hide a lamp under a bowl if you want it to chase away darkness. You set it on a stand so that it can be seen (Matthew 5). In the same way, a city on a hill is visible for miles around. Driving northeast through New Jersey, the skyline of Manhattan comes into view long before you reach the George Washington Bridge. It may still be a great distance away, but the city stands out against the sky to draw people to its presence.

Healthcare in the United States is currently shrouded in darkness. Compared to ten of the world's wealthiest nations, America spends a significant amount more on healthcare. You would think that extra investment would yield a higher return. Unfortunately, the opposite is true. Those other nations easily outperform America producing better health for their citizens. We have more expensive healthcare and fewer healthy citizens. Even worse—hospital errors are the number three cause of death in America today. All the statistics tell us it's getting worse. The healthcare darkness is spreading.

Even as we spend more on healthcare, our life expectancy is dropping. Among white Americans in 2020, the year the COVID pandemic hit, life expectancy dropped by over a year. But for Black and Hispanic Americans, it dropped by three years. Imagine losing three years—so much can be accomplished in three years.

But that's only part of the story. There is a huge gap in life expectancy between the wealthiest Americans and the poorest. In New Orleans, there's a twenty-five-year gap in life expectancy between neighborhoods that are separated by only four miles. For people living in the poorest neighborhood, their average life expectancy is fifty-seven. In the richer neighborhood, residents can expect to live to eighty-three. One comparison of Chicago neighborhoods saw a *thirty*-year gap in life expectancy. Thirty years of life. During the nineteenth century, thirty years was often a lifetime. Inequity is the ultimate darkness.

US healthcare is a business of just under four *trillion* dollars. US healthcare is the largest business in the world. And what do these huge US healthcare companies do to maximize their profits? They invest in the wealthy neighborhoods, where people have expensive healthcare plans and sufficient money to pay for high-cost procedures. They pull out of poor neighborhoods where they lose money on people who are dependent on government-subsidized insurance.

The corporations that control healthcare in America are exacerbating this inequity. In every city in America, these large healthcare systems are consolidating options available to people, wiping out competition and raising prices. This is monopolistic behavior by beautiful people stuck in a broken and poorly incentivized system.

They only make money when people get sick. Stuck in this system, they feel they can't change. The system's technology, compensation, and structure achieve the opposite of what America needs—better outcomes at lower cost while equalizing health inequities.

As we grow and become more of a force in healthcare, more and more of these beautiful people are either joining us at ChenMed, choosing to partner with us in some capacity, or gravitating to one of the companies doing work similar to ours. These partnerships are how we will reach a broader population that will use our ChenMed centers as a model for what good healthcare looks like. By ourselves, we can only reach so many. But with our example and partnerships, we are reaching so many more.

Dad was once asked, "Why do you build these beautiful centers in sad, forlorn places?"

"We need to bring light and hope to them," he answered.

We continue to put our centers in the most underserved, most difficult, most challenging places, with the greatest lifespan disparity. We plan to place them, as they're needed and as we're able, in every city in America.

And we always start by taking care of the oldest, the poorest, the sickest. As often as possible, we hire people from these areas as support staff, giving them jobs and a purpose. We also import the best doctors and leaders to run our centers. We identify and help the longest-serving leaders in these communities get healthy and strong so they can improve their neighborhoods. We've recently initiated center-based giving—a percentage of the profits from our centers goes back into the communities for improvement. And we're testing empowering leaders in these areas to identify faith-based communities where the best work is being done.

The first half of our vision says that we want to be "America's leading primary care provider." We're on our way to getting there. But the second half of our vision is the really hard part: "transforming care of the neediest populations." It means changing a four-trillion-dollar colossus—the healthcare industry—and addressing inequities in the way that industry operates. To do that, we need to have thousands of ChenMed centers across America.

In 2020 *Fortune* magazine named us one of their fifty-three international "Change the World" organizations. We were the only healthcare provider that made their list. The magazine highlighted the current problems of inequity and low value of American healthcare while recognizing our lower hospitalizations and equitable care for the neediest among us.

As of this writing, and as fast as we are growing, value-based care providers offer less than one percent of America's primary care. Which means we have a long way to go to fulfill our vision of transforming care for the neediest populations. But we've never let a long distance in front of us stop us from embarking on a journey, a journey we believe we have a moral imperative to make.

We're a family who've experienced what it means to struggle, to be poor, to know the battles people wage for quality care within the healthcare system. We've seen miraculous change occur, with doors opening before us that we never dreamed possible. We've been able to attract mission-driven people to join us, people with a heart for the needy and vulnerable among us.

Now we're a force leading the charge in a healthcare revolution, using primary care as the main beacon of light shining in the darkness. We're doing that one patient at a time, one primary care physician at a time, one care team at a time, one center, one community, one city on a hill at a time.

Along with making *Fortune*'s list of fifty-three "Change the World" organizations, in 2021 we were named by *Newsweek* one of "The Most Loved Companies in America." We were at number thirty-six and the top-ranked company in healthcare. We were selected as "The Best Place to Work for IT" and certified as "A Great Place to Work."

We continue to expand services for our team members through ChenMed Cares, and recently we introduced TeamCare, an opportunity for our ChenMed employees to experience the same VIP care we give our patients. We're also launching Youth Impact Centers in communities we serve, designed to provide inner city kids with physical, mental, academic, and spiritual support to help them reach their full God-given potential.

In the coming years, our intention is to open hundreds of new centers, hiring thousands of primary care physicians along with tens of thousands of business leaders and care team members. We challenge ourselves to grow faster while improving service, improving outcomes, and improving culture for our patients and the communities in which they live. We know it can be done because we're watching it happen year after year from the forefront of this healthcare revolution.

At a *minimum*, we should experience quadruple growth over the next three years. While we've talked primarily about our work in the United States, we will continue our thirty-plus-year commitment to medical missions in Nicaragua and support physicians there who serve twenty-five communities. We have doctors in Uganda whom we're training and supporting. We can envision our healthcare revolution spreading throughout Central America, Africa, and the rest of the world. We plan on staying on the "Change the World" list for a long, long time.

That is our hope, our desire, our commitment to America. And in doing that, we truly will bring light to darkness and change the world.

# ACKNOWLEDGMENTS

WE ONCE BELIEVED creating a book was a lonely and solitary effort. We were wrong. The phrase "It takes a village" applies to writing a book as well as raising children.

All six of us —Dad and Mom, Chris and Stephanie, Gordon and Jessica—are indebted to the following professionals for helping us tell our story.

To start off, our family wants to give a special thank-you to Jeff Opperman for his friendship, perseverance, and leadership to help make this book possible. We are forever grateful for how you love our family and support our mission in this unique way.

Kevin Anderson, Cole Gustafson, Freddy Richardson, Stephen Power, Amanda Ayers Barnett, and Metta Sáma from Kevin Anderson & Associates: Your expertise and patience shepherding a couple of inexperienced authors through the writing process created a far better story than we could have ever told ourselves.

Jonathan Merkh, Jennifer Gingerich, Lauren Ward, and the incredible team at Forefront Books. Somehow, you took our manuscript and created a real honest-to-goodness book in less than five months! But more than that, you recognized the flaws in our healthcare system and the importance of bringing better health to more underserved Americans. We thank you on their behalf.

Vicky Durkin, Vicky Terrier, Evelin Rodriguez, and Jennifer Andia at ChenMed. Job descriptions often say "other duties as assigned," but helping us write and publish a book was the last thing on all our minds when you came aboard. The love, accountability, and passion you've demonstrated for this project has exceeded our wildest expectations.

Finally, we thank God for His mercy and grace, for the opportunity to serve Him in such a meaningful way, and for guiding us on our book-writing journey. *The Calling* isn't just a book title. We believe His calling put us on a path to transform healthcare and help make ChenMed America's leading primary care provider, transforming care for the neediest populations. Our lives have been transformed through Christ's truth and love, and we pray that this book can allow others to experience the same.